Frugal

Living

Easy Ways to Spend Less and Save More

(Step by Step Guide to a Frugal Life With Financial Freedom, Debt Free and Fulfillment)

Dirk McNutt

Published By **Windy Dawson**

Dirk McNutt

All Rights Reserved

Frugal Living: Easy Ways to Spend Less and Save More (Step by Step Guide to a Frugal Life With Financial Freedom, Debt Free and Fulfillment)

ISBN 978-1-7776902-6-7

Legal & Disclaimer

Table Of Contents

Chapter 1: The Power Of Budgeting

Budgeting is a powerful device with a view to can help you take manipulates of your price range, achieve your financial goals, and live a more financially normal lifestyles. A budget is a financial plan that lets you song your earnings and costs, and to make certain which you're spending your cash in a way that aligns along with your priorities and desires. Here are 5 academic paragraphs on a manner to create and stay with a charge variety.

The first step in developing a price range is to determine your earnings and prices. Start with the aid of creating a listing of all your sources of income, which incorporates your profits or any aspect hustles you've got got. Then, make a list of all of your month-to-month prices, which include payments, groceries, transportation, and entertainment. Be superb to include all of your expenses, even small ones like a everyday espresso or snacks. This will offer you with a clean photograph of your financial situation.

Once you have got were given a listing of your income and prices, it is time to set a price range. Start by using using way of prioritizing your prices, so that you can allocate your earnings as a result. For example, prioritize essential expenses alongside lease or loan, utilities, and groceries. Then, set sensible finances for discretionary prices like ingesting out or shopping for. Remember that your price range must permit for a few amusing and enjoyment, so do not experience like you need to reduce out all your non-crucial fees.

To keep on with your rate variety, it is vital to music your spending. Keep a file of your charges, both on paper or the usage of a budgeting app. This will let you look in which you are spending your cash and discover regions in which you might be overspending. You can then regulate your price range subsequently to make sure which you live on track.

Another key element of sticking in your charge range is making plans for unexpected fees. No rely how well you recommend, unexpected prices can and could arise. Make wonderful to allocate some coins for emergencies, so that you do now not should dip into different areas of your fee range while sudden fees rise up.

Remember that budgeting is an ongoing system. Your earnings, charges, and economic desires will likely trade through the years, so it's miles essential to test and modify your fee range regularly. By making budgeting a dependancy and staying centered to your financial dreams, you could take manage of your rate variety and collect the economic freedom and safety you deserve.

One way to make budgeting much less tough is to apply cash envelopes. With this device, you withdraw coins for every budget beauty and placed it in a chosen envelope. You then simplest use the coins in that envelope for that elegance. This may want to make it less complex to music your spending and keep on along side your price range, as you physical see how heaps money you have got got were given left in every envelope.

Another tip for sticking in your rate range is to discover techniques to reduce expenses. Look for gives, reductions, and coupons to preserve money on groceries, family items, and different fees. You also can take into account negotiating decrease fees on payments and services or switching to a less luxurious issuer. Small monetary monetary financial savings can add up quick and help you live interior your price variety.

It's additionally critical to be flexible together collectively together with your charge range. Life takes region, and every so often surprising expenses get up. If you cross over price variety one month, do now not get discouraged. Review your spending, alter your rate range as wished, and get lower back on route the subsequent month. Remember that budgeting is an extended-time period technique, and the occasional slip-up does no longer mean you have got failed.

Celebrate your budgeting successes. When you purchased a financial savings intention or maintain on with your budget for a wonderful time period, take some time to famend and have a very good time your development. This can help preserve you impacted and targeted to your economic goals. Budgeting may be difficult inside the beginning, but with exercising and persistence, it is able to grow to be a addiction that permits you advantage your dreams and stay a extra exceptional life.

Budgeting also can sound dull, but it's truely one of the only machine to your monetary arsenal. By growing a price range, you'll be capable of see in which your cash goes and ensure it's going for walks for you, not towards you. And who is privy to? Maybe you'll even find out that you've been spending a fortune on avocado toast and can redirect the ones finances to a few issue extra essential, like a journey to Bali.

So, how do you create a rate variety? Start with the useful resource of tracking your spending for some weeks to get an idea of wherein your cash is going. Then, make a list of your month-to-month charges, like rent, groceries, and Netflix (due to the reality allow's be actual, that's a need). Next, set a rate variety for every magnificence and maintain on with it. It can also moreover moreover take some trial and errors to discover the right balance, but take into account us, it's in truth really really worth it.

One of the keys to sticking to a rate range is to make it amusing! Think of creative strategies to reduce expenses, like having a "no-spend" day wherein you don't spend any cash in any respect, or tough your buddies to look who can find out the great offers at the grocery keep. And while you do splurge, make certain it's some aspect you definitely rate – like a live performance charge rate ticket or a flowery dinner – instead of absolutely mindlessly swiping your credit score card.

Budgeting additionally may be a terrific manner to bring together healthful financial conduct. When you see how an lousy lot you're saving each month, it's a great deal less hard to stand up to the urge to buy that new pair of footwear or decorate to the contemporary iPhone. Plus, by way of using sticking to a rate variety, you'll be capable of attain your economic goals faster, whether or not or now not that's paying off debt or saving for a down rate on a residence.

Finally, don't forget that budgeting isn't always approximately deprivation – it's about prioritizing the matters that take into account number to you. So, if excursion is critical to you, make sure to set aside cash for that dream excursion. And in case you're a foodie at coronary heart, don't be afraid to splurge on a elaborate meal every now and then. The secret is to find a balance that works for you and your monetary goals. So pass forth and rate range like a md!

Eliminating Debt: Strategies for Paying Off Credit Cards and Loans

Eliminating debt is an important step toward accomplishing financial freedom and protection. The longer you convey debt, the more you pay in hobby and the harder it's miles to acquire your economic desires. Here are strategies for paying off credit score cards and loans.

The first step in paying off debt is to prevent including to it. This way setting away credit score score gambling gambling playing cards and no longer taking away any more loans. Focus on residing internal your method and reducing your expenses where possible. This will assist you keep away from which includes more debt to your current balances.

The next step is to prioritize your debt bills. Start via method of making a listing of all of your debts, which includes the balance, interest price, and minimal rate. Then, determine which debt to pay off first. There are famous techniques for this: the snowball method and the avalanche technique. The snowball method involves paying off your smallest stability first, at the same time as the avalanche method consists of paying off the debt with the first-rate hobby price first. Whichever approach you choose, the key's to stay centered and devoted to paying off your money owed.

Another technique for paying off debt is to negotiate lower interest charges. Call your credit score score card organizations or loan companies and ask if they could lower your hobby rate. If you have got a excellent price facts, they may be willing to artwork with you to decrease your rate. This allow you to maintain cash on interest and repay your debt quicker.

Consider consolidating your debt proper right into a unmarried loan or credit score score card with a decrease hobby fee. This will will let you simplify your debt bills and keep coins on interest. Be positive to do your research and compare outstanding consolidation alternatives earlier than making a decision. You don't want to become with a better interest price or hidden fees so that it will make your debt situation worse.

Eliminating debt takes effort and time, however it's miles actually worth it. By using the ones techniques and staying centered in your financial dreams, you can take manage of your debt and gain the financial freedom and safety you deserve.

Another beneficial method for paying off debt is to increase your earnings. Look for methods to earn extra cash, which includes taking on a element-time technique, selling gadgets you now not need, or presenting offerings to others. Use the extra income to make more payments in the direction of your debt. This will assist you to repay your money owed quicker and reduce the amount of hobby you pay over the years.

It's moreover essential to stay stimulated at the equal time as paying off debt. Set unique dreams and song your development. Celebrate small victories alongside the way, along with paying off a single credit score card or making a bigger charge than commonplace. Visualize the benefits of being debt-unfastened, together with having extra cash for adventure or being able to save for a down rate on a domestic.

Another tip is to avoid comparing your self to others. It's easy to revel in like you're falling inside the returned of even as you notice friends or circle of relatives people with big incomes or less debt. Remember that everyone's economic scenario is precise, and recognition for your personal desires and improvement. Be glad with the stairs you are taking to remove debt and gather your financial dreams.

Finally, it is crucial to have a plan for staying debt-loose as soon as you have got paid off your balances. Consider developing a charge range, constructing an emergency fund, and putting in region computerized financial financial savings contributions. These steps allow you to avoid falling lower returned into debt and keep your financial stability over the long time.

Paying off debt calls for problem, attention, and perseverance. By the use of a aggregate of strategies which encompass prioritizing your payments, negotiating decrease hobby prices, and increasing your profits, you could take away your debt and attain financial freedom. Stay brought on, keep away from comparisons to others, and make a plan for staying debt-free. With tough work and dedication, you could take control of your fee variety and construct a brighter monetary future.

Ah, debt – the closing buzzkill. But fear no longer, my financially savvy pal! With a piece method and backbone, you can kick that debt to the reduce and begin residing your high-quality lifestyles. So allow's get to it and start putting off that pesky debt.

Make superb you have a listing of all your debts, together with credit score score playing cards, loans, and each exceptional extraordinary balances. Once you have got were given were given a clear picture of what you owe, prioritize your money owed primarily based totally on interest fees and minimal payments. Focus on paying off the very quality hobby fee debts first, even as however making minimum payments at the others.

One of the only strategies for paying off debt is the "snowball approach." Start through paying off your smallest debt first, at the equal time as making minimum bills at the others. Once you've paid off that debt, take the cash you have been setting inside the direction of it and upload it for your price for the following smallest debt. Keep snowballing your payments till all your money owed are paid off – it's like a economic endeavor of Jenga!

Another way to remove debt is to consolidate your high-hobby money owed proper right into a unmarried, decrease hobby fee mortgage. This should make it less difficult to govern your payments and probable prevent coins on interest prices. Just make certain to study the quality print and understand any prices or outcomes related to the mortgage.

Finally, don't forget that paying off debt is a marathon, not a sprint. It may additionally moreover furthermore take the time and strive, but the feeling of monetary freedom at the same time as you subsequently grow to be debt-unfastened is properly worth it. And who knows? Maybe ultimately you'll be able to cope with your self to that dream excursion or splurge on that clothier purse without a hint of guilt. So maintain chipping away at that debt, my friend – you've were given this!

Chapter 2: Saving On Housing

Housing is often taken into consideration one in all of the maximum essential expenses in someone's price range, but there are processes to preserve coins on lease or loan fees. Here are four advice-toned paragraphs with suggestions for decreasing your housing fees.

First, bear in mind downsizing your living area. Moving to a smaller apartment or residence can prevent loads of bucks in step with month on rent or mortgage payments. Downsizing may additionally moreover help you reduce particular housing-associated fees which consist of utilities, safety, and coverage. Be first-rate to cautiously recollect your dreams and lifestyle at the same time as selecting a smaller area, and remember to detail in moving prices.

Another manner to store on housing is to negotiate your lease or loan. If you are an superb tenant or borrower with a sturdy rate statistics, your landlord or lender may be inclined to barter your lease or mortgage charge. Be nice to do your research and are available organized with facts on condo or loan charges to your location. A easy phone name or meeting along with your landlord or lender ought to result in big monetary financial savings over time.

Consider taking on a roommate or renting out a part of your house. This can help you offset the rate of your housing expenses and decrease the financial burden. Be sure to carefully vet capability roommates and establish clean expectations and obstacles to keep away from conflicts or misunderstandings.

Look for opportunities to earn greater earnings via your housing scenario. If you personal your own home, undergo in mind renting out a room on Airbnb or renting out your parking space. If you are renting, look for methods to earn cash again on lease payments, which includes through cashback apps or credit rating gambling playing cards.

These small earnings streams can add up over time and assist you shop on your housing charges.

There are many strategies to maintain coins on housing expenses. Consider downsizing, negotiating your rent or loan, taking over a roommate, or incomes more income via your housing scenario. With a chunk creativity and try, you may lessen your housing prices and free up extra money to acquire your economic desires.

In addition to the ones strategies, there are various other strategies to shop coins on housing costs. One way is to search for discounts or precise programs. For instance, a few towns offer tax incentives for house owners who make electricity-green enhancements, at the identical time as others provide condominium help packages for low-income citizens. Be positive to investigate to be had alternatives in your vicinity and take advantage of any opportunities that will let you keep coins in your housing expenses.

Another approach is to look for procedures to lessen your software costs. Simple adjustments, which include putting in strength-inexperienced slight bulbs or taking shorter showers, assist you to save coins for your month-to-month utility payments. You also can be capable of negotiate a decrease charge in conjunction with your utility company or switch to a business enterprise that gives better expenses or incentives.

Another tip is to keep away from overspending on domestic enhancements or furnishings. While it's far tempting to splurge on a latest couch or kitchen redecorate, the ones fees can rapid add up and boom your housing charges. Instead, recognition on making small modifications or DIY responsibilities with the intention to will let you keep cash and decorate your residing place.

Finally, it is critical to examine your housing expenses often and make changes as wished. This consists of reviewing your lease or mortgage payments, software payments, and different housing-related charges to make sure that you're not overspending. Use a budgeting app or spreadsheet to music your fees and discover areas wherein you could make adjustments to preserve coins.

In summary, there are various strategies to preserve cash on housing prices, which includes searching out discounts or special applications, decreasing your software program expenses, heading off overspending on domestic upgrades or furnishings, and frequently reviewing your charges. By taking a proactive method to managing your housing prices, you could reduce your economic burden and loose up extra money to gain your financial desires.

Let's face it – housing is really considered one of the maximum vital costs we'll ever have. But don't allow your rent or mortgage payments deliver you down! With a touch creativity and determination, you can find strategies to store coins and make your housing expenses more capacity.

If you're renting, strive negotiating your rent together together together with your landlord. It can also sound intimidating, but you never understand till you attempt! Highlight your correct condominium information and provide to sign an prolonged hire in change for a lower hire. Who is aware about? Your landlord can also admire the steadiness and be inclined to art work with you.

Finally, don't be afraid to get creative alongside aspect your housing alternatives. Tiny houses, houseboats, or even yurts are becoming an increasing number of well-known as inexpensive and sustainable housing alternatives. And who is aware of? Living in a very specific and unconventional space can also moreover absolutely spark your creativity and reason new adventures. So float forth and maintain on housing, my friend – the opportunities are endless!

Cutting Utility Bills: Ways to Save on Electricity, Water, and Gas

Let's face it, nobody likes paying their utility bills. But there are methods to save coins and decrease the ache of these monthly costs.

First, do not forget bribing your roommates or circle of relatives people to be more strength-conscious. For example, offer to pay for a night out or do their chores in the event that they bear in thoughts to expose off the lighting once they depart a room. You may also moreover even create a rewards chart with stickers and gold stars for folks who usually make electricity-saving choices. Just do no longer permit the bribery rate extra than the real economic financial financial savings on your utility invoice!

Another funny manner to keep on software program payments is to reveal it into a game. You can project your family or roommates to look who can take the shortest bathe or who can unplug the most devices in advance than leaving the house. Set up a nice opposition with prizes for the winner, together with bragging rights or a selfmade trophy. Who knew saving coins may be so a laugh?

Beyond the amusing and video video games, there are numerous sensible methods to reduce your software program payments.

First and essential, you need to switch to power-green domestic equipment and slight bulbs. Energy-green home gadget can notably reduce your strength usage, on the identical time as LED light bulbs burn up to 75% lots less electricity than conventional bulbs. Though those home equipment and bulbs might cost more to start with, they'll in the long run pay for themselves inside the shape of decrease application bills.

Another tip is to adjust your thermostat. During the summer time, decorate your thermostat some tiers and use fans to chill your house. During the wintry weather, lower your thermostat a few tiers and use greater blankets to live heat. A programmable thermostat will let you automate those changes and reduce your strength utilization with out sacrificing comfort.

You need to moreover look for ways to lessen your water utilization. This consists of solving leaky taps, taking shorter showers, and washing most effective entire masses of laundry or dishes. You can also set up low-glide showerheads and faucets, as a way to allow you to shop as a whole lot as 50% on your water invoice.

In addition, you want to keep in mind the usage of herbal slight as masses as feasible. Open your blinds or curtains inside the path of the day to permit sunlight hours in and avoid turning on unnecessary lights. You can also paint your partitions with light shades or add mirrors to mirror natural light and brighten your space without the use of power.

You want to continuously be privy to your power usage. Unplug appliances and electronics even as you're not using them, and avoid leaving lighting fixtures on in empty rooms. You can also use electricity strips to with out troubles turn off more than one gadgets right away, and remember placing a reminder for your cellular telephone or calendar to regularly take a look at your application bills and music your improvement.

By following those suggestions and being conscious of your utility usage, you can notably reduce your monthly software bills and shop coins through the years. With a touch try and interest to detail, you can make lowering software bills a everyday a part of your budget and monetary planning.

Did you recognize that turning off the lighting fixtures while you depart a room isn't always handiest a super way to keep on energy, however moreover a excellent manner to avoid being wrong for a ghost? You'll thank me later while your own family and buddies save you walking out of the residence in terror each time they see a mild flicker on and off.

Want to shop on water bills? Start taking shorter showers! Not quality will you preserve water, however you'll moreover get a notable exercising trying to wash all the cleaning cleansing cleaning soap off in report time. Who needs a fitness center club whilst you may have a clean judgment of proper and incorrect and biceps of metal?

If you're bored with paying exorbitant gas payments, attempt the usage of public transportation or carpooling with buddies. Not best will you shop money, but you'll additionally have the brought benefit of becoming the social butterfly of the place of work. Who needs a vehicle at the same time as you may have a whole new network of friends?

Did you recognise that turning off your laptop whilst you're now not the use of it may prevent as masses as $75 per three hundred and sixty five days on electricity payments? Plus, you'll keep away from the anxiety of annoying approximately your computer being hacked with the aid of nefarious internet trolls. Trust me, your pockets and your sanity will thank you.

Want to preserve on water payments even as moreover channeling your internal superhero? Try putting in a rain barrel to build up rainwater for watering flowers and washing your car. You'll feel like Captain Planet each time you use it, and your pockets will thanks for the more money in your pocket.

Finally, if you're in reality essential approximately saving on strength bills, put money into a few solar panels! Not simplest will you preserve cash, but you'll moreover have the pleasure of understanding which you're doing all your component to maintain the planet. Plus, you'll get to brag to all your pals about how you're essentially a contemporary-day-day Captain Planet.

Chapter 3: Strategies for Reducing Food Costs

Food is one of the maximum awesome fees in a circle of relatives rate range. However, with a few simple techniques, you may maintain cash on groceries with out sacrificing the first-rate or amount of your meals:

The first step to saving on groceries is to plan your food in advance. Make a list of what you need in advance than you purchase groceries, and stick with it. This will let you avoid impulse buys and decrease meals waste via only shopping for what you want. You can also use coupons, keep classified ads, and on line gives to keep cash on precise items.

Another manner to shop on groceries is to shop for regular or store-brand merchandise. Many keep-logo merchandise are just as pinnacle as the decision-emblem alternatives, however charge considerably less. You can also buy in bulk for non-perishable items, along side rice, pasta, and canned items, that may prevent cash ultimately.

You have to also preserve in thoughts looking for produce it's miles in season. Fruits and vegetables which is probably in season tend to be plenty less luxurious and more energizing than those which is probably out of season. You also can buy frozen culmination and veggies, which can be regularly less luxurious than easy produce and might last longer to your freezer.

You have to learn how to cook dinner from scratch. Pre-made and processed food have a propensity to be more costly than selfmade alternatives. You can save cash thru shopping for raw substances and cooking your food from scratch. This moreover may be a more wholesome option, as you may control the outstanding and quantity of the substances you use.

By planning your meals earlier, shopping for not unusual or maintain-emblem products, deciding on seasonal produce, and cooking from scratch, you can hold cash on groceries and reduce your trendy meals prices. These strategies additionally can help you make greater healthy meals alternatives and decrease food waste, this is right to your wallet and the environment. With a hint attempt and hobby to detail, you may make saving on groceries a everyday part of your monetary planning.

I'll give up this financial ruin with the tale of a chum, Emily who had genuinely graduated from university and commenced out her first way. She have become excited to have a constant profits however changed into greatly surprised while she found out how an entire lot she have turn out to be spending on groceries each month.

Emily had commonly taken into consideration herself to be a frugal man or woman, however she could not appear to preserve her meals costs below manipulate. She knew she needed to discover a manner to save on groceries, so she were given down to research a few techniques for decreasing her meals costs.

The first detail Emily did modified into to make a meal plan for the week. She commenced out through the use of taking stock of what she already had in her pantry and fridge, and then made a list of the food she desired to prepare for the week. She additionally made high-quality to include a few easy-to-prepare meals for nights even as she grow to be too tired to prepare dinner.

Next, Emily started out buying with a listing and fixed to it. She moreover determined out to avoid impulse purchases thru no longer purchasing on the identical time as she have emerge as hungry. She found that via way of purchasing this manner, she became capable of lessen her grocery invoice with the useful resource of almost 20%.

Emily moreover placed that she want to save coins with the beneficial aid of searching for in bulk. She started out out out buying items like rice, pasta, and canned devices in huge portions and storing them in her pantry. She moreover commenced out buying meat in bulk and freezing it in smaller quantities, which saved her money and reduced food waste.

Another technique Emily used emerge as to take benefit of income and coupons. She signed up for her community grocery keep's rewards utility, which gave her access to distinct gives and coupons. She furthermore checked the weekly classified ads to appearance which devices have been on sale and planned her food around the ones gadgets.

Finally, Emily started to test with cooking from scratch. She decided to make her very personal bread, yogurt, or even pasta. By doing this, she modified into able to keep coins and manage the materials in her meals.

In the surrender, Emily have become able to reduce her grocery bill thru greater than 30%. She turn out to be surprised at how lots cash she became capable of store with the aid of the usage of making smooth changes to her looking for and cooking conduct. She found out that saving on groceries did now not should be difficult, and that with a chunk making plans and attempt, anyone may additionally need to do it.

Are you uninterested in overspending on groceries? Try purchasing for in bulk! Not best will you shop cash, however you'll moreover revel in like a md wearing out your supersized luggage of cereal and lavatory paper. Who needs a gymnasium membership at the same time as you can construct arm muscular tissues sporting a ten-pound bag of rice?

Want to keep coins on groceries at the same time as furthermore feeling like a culinary wizard? Try meal prepping! You'll experience like a magician conjuring up scrumptious meals out of skinny air, and also you'll store cash with the aid of not having to reserve takeout each night time time. Who dreams a private chef whilst you will be your very own kitchen magician?

Are you tired of throwing out expired meals? Try freezing your leftovers! You'll keep coins thru way of no longer wasting food, and also you'll also have the delight of understanding which you're an eco-friendly superhero. Who goals a cape whilst you may have a freezer entire of perfectly preserved leftovers?

Want to preserve cash on groceries whilst additionally supporting your nearby farmers? Try searching for at your nearby farmers' marketplace! You'll feel like a contemporary-day Robin Hood, assisting small businesses and community farmers even as additionally saving cash on produce. Who wishes a huge field grocery hold while you may be a close-by hero?

Are you tired of buying emblem-call merchandise that fee an arm and a leg? Try searching for hold-brand merchandise! You'll hold cash without sacrificing high-quality, and also you'll moreover have the delight of understanding which you're a savvy client. Who needs a fancy label whilst you may have more money to your pockets?

Finally, if you're excessive about saving money on groceries, attempt growing your very very very own produce! You'll save coins, get some smooth air and sunshine, and have the satisfaction of information that you're a self-sufficient superhero. Who goals a inexperienced thumb when you may have a inexperienced pockets?

Chapter 4: Cutting Transportation Costs

Transportation prices may be a huge a part of a circle of relatives price range, whether or not you very own a car or depend upon public transit. Fortunately, there are many methods to lessen transportation costs and keep cash. Here are some strategies that will help you reduce your transportation expenses:

Reduce your fuel charges - One of the simplest approaches to keep on gas is to power an awful lot less. You can carpool with co-employees, use public transit, or perhaps stroll or motorbike for quick journeys. Another way to keep on gasoline is to stress extra efficiently thru warding off surprising acceleration and braking, retaining a regular tempo, and preserving your tires inflated to the fine pressure. You can also bear in thoughts the usage of a fuel rewards credit rating rating card to earn coins returned or factors to your gas purchases.

Maintain your vehicle properly - Regular automobile preservation will will let you keep away from highly-priced preservation and beautify your car's fuel overall performance. This includes converting your oil and air clear out, rotating your tires, and preserving your engine tuned up. Keeping your vehicle easy and free of extra weight can also help you shop on gasoline.

Take advantage of public transit reductions - If you use public transit, ensure to check if there are any discounts available. Many towns provide discounted fares for university youngsters, seniors, and coffee-profits citizens. Some employers additionally provide transit advantages to their employees, together with pre-tax payroll deductions or sponsored transit passes.

Consider automobile-sharing or renting - If you best want a car sometimes, you may be capable of keep cash with the resource of using a car-sharing carrier like Zipcar or renting a vehicle from a issuer like Turo. This can be a fee-effective alternative to proudly owning a car, mainly if you live in a city in which parking is luxurious or tough to find out. Plus, you'll keep cash on gasoline and car maintenance with the resource of not using as loads.

By enforcing these techniques, you may lessen your transportation prices and unfastened up extra money for extraordinary costs. Whether you very private a vehicle or use public transit, there are various techniques to maintain cash and enhance your normal financial well-being.

Cutting transportation prices is an critical step for human beings and agencies to improve their monetary health, increase profitability, decorate competitiveness, and reduce their environmental effect. By locating approaches to reduce transportation charges, people and corporations can optimize their belongings and achieve their financial and sustainability desires.

Gas costs may be a extremely good price for drivers. One way to preserve on gasoline is to electricity more efficiently. Avoiding competitive using, retaining your tires well inflated, and using cruise control at the dual carriageway can all enhance your gasoline financial device. It might not seem like masses, but over the years the ones small modifications can upload as tons as large financial savings.

Regular car preservation can save you luxurious renovation down the road. To shop on automobile upkeep, make certain to conform together with your car's maintenance time table and perform easy maintenance obligations like checking your oil and air easy out. If you're no longer snug doing those duties your self, bear in mind finding a reliable mechanic who received't overcharge you for unnecessary preservation.

Public transit can be a price-powerful and inexperienced manner to get around. Taking the bus or educate can save you cash on gas and parking expenses, in addition to lessen your carbon footprint. Many towns provide discounted passes for common riders, so make certain to do your research to find out the awesome deal.

Carpooling is a few different manner to keep coins on transportation. By sharing the charge of gasoline and tolls with others, you could appreciably reduce your costs. Plus, carpooling can be a exceptional way to fulfill new people and decrease web site site visitors congestion.

If you live in a metropolis with a bike-first-class infrastructure, biking may be a outstanding way to keep cash on transportation and stay in form. Just ensure to put money into a splendid motorbike lock and observe internet site traffic legal pointers to stay stable on the street.

Finally, recollect downsizing to a greater fuel-green automobile in case you often power extended distances or have a long adventure. Hybrid and electric powered motors can save you coins on gas and decrease your carbon footprint. While they may have a better in advance fee, the prolonged-term monetary financial savings may be big.

Chapter 5: How to Find Deals and Discounts on Everyday Purchases

Smart purchasing is a way that could help people and households hold coins on regular purchases. The approach entails the use of pretty some gadget and techniques to locate gives, reductions, and coupons that permit you to get the maximum from your coins. Here are some pointers on the manner to discover gives and discounts on ordinary purchases.

Use Coupons and Promo Codes: One of the best techniques to shop coins on ordinary purchases is with the beneficial resource of the use of coupons and promo codes. These can be placed in severa locations, which incorporates in-keep flyers, online coupon net websites, or through e mail newsletters. Many stores furthermore offer their non-public loyalty applications that provide reductions and promotions to ordinary purchasers.

Compare Prices: Another powerful manner to keep cash when shopping for is to assess costs throughout one in every of a type stores. Use rate contrast net web sites or apps to discover the amazing offers on a specific product. You also can test out nearby advertisements to peer which shops have sales at the objects you need.

Take Advantage of Sales and Clearance Events: Most shops provide regular profits and clearance sports, in which they mark down merchandise to make room for logo spanking new inventory. These occasions may be a excellent possibility to snag devices you want at a fragment of the ordinary price. Keep a be careful for shop emails, flyers, and social media posts to stay informed approximately upcoming income and discounts.

Buy in Bulk: Buying in bulk is a few other exquisite way to store coins on everyday purchases. Items like non-perishable meals, cleaning factors, and toiletries can be offered in large portions at a reduction. Just make certain to calculate the rate regular with unit to ensure you have become the exceptional deal.

In end, smart purchasing is an critical technique to save cash on everyday purchases. By the use of coupons, comparing expenses, taking advantage of income and clearance occasions, and purchasing for in bulk, humans and households can stretch their fee range and get greater out of their coins. With a bit little bit of making plans and strive, in reality all and sundry can be a clever customer and maintain huge on normal purchases.

Utilize Cashback and Reward Programs: Many credit score card groups and on-line shops offer cashback and praise programs to be able to let you earn cash another time to your purchases. By the use of the ones programs, you can earn rewards elements or cash again for every dollar you spend, which may be redeemed for future purchases or announcement credit. Some shops additionally provide rewards programs that offer one-of-a-kind discounts or unfastened items to normal customers.

Shop During Off-Season: Buying seasonal gadgets all through low season can prevent a huge amount of money. For instance, shopping for winter clothes within the summer season, or buying outside tools inside the wintry climate season can motive extensive savings. By buying out of season, you can take benefit of clearance earnings and discounted charges, and maintain cash on gadgets you want.

Negotiate with Sellers: When making bigger purchases like furniture, domestic tool or electronics, it is regularly possible to negotiate with sellers for a higher rate. Don't be afraid to invite for a discount, in particular in case you're paying in cash or developing a bulk buy. You also can search for open area or ground models which is probably discounted because of getting used as display fashions.

Don't Buy More Than You Need: It's easy to get caught up in the excitement of a sale or reduce fee and grow to be looking for greater than you really need. Before creating a purchase, consider whether or not you really want the object, or if it's far only a good buy. If you're not extraordinary, take some time to reflect onconsideration on it in advance than making a decision. Avoid shopping for stuff you may not use, as it will best result in muddle and wasted cash.

In summary, clever purchasing includes a aggregate of strategies that will help you shop cash on regular purchases. By using coupons, evaluating prices, taking benefit of earnings and clearance sports, purchasing for in bulk, utilising cashback and praise packages, shopping for low season, negotiating with dealers, and now not looking for greater than you want, you could maximize your economic economic financial savings and stretch your finances. With a touch little bit of strive, each person can end up a smart purchaser and shop big on regular purchases.

Are you bored with paying entire price for the whole thing? Then it's time to emerge as a clever consumer! Don't be fooled via flashy classified ads or fancy packaging. Do your studies, have a observe opinions, and have a look at fees to discover the super deal. Who desires to be a fool at the same time as you will be a savvy consumer?

Want to preserve coins on groceries? Try shopping for in bulk! Not first-rate will you keep coins, however you'll also have the introduced benefit of feeling like a superhero on every occasion you lug a huge bag of rice home from the shop. Who needs a non-public instructor on the identical time as you could bring luggage of groceries?

If you're a frequent on-line customer, strive using browser extensions like Honey or Rakuten to routinely observe discounts and discounts at checkout. It's like having your personal private buying assistant! Who desires a private purchaser if you have a pc?

Always check for earnings and clearance objects earlier than making a buy. You in no way recognize at the same time as you'll discover a hidden gem at a reduced price. Plus, it's constantly pleasing to apprehend that you purchased a awesome deal. Who desires to be rich while you can be a good deal hunter?

Consider signing up for loyalty packages or e-mail newsletters from your desired shops. You'll be the primary to realize approximately sales and discounts, and you may even get one-of-a-type gives just for being a member. Who desires to be an intruder whilst you'll be a VIP?

Finally, don't be afraid to negotiate! Whether you're purchasing for a car or a bit of furniture, it in no way hurts to invite for a higher price. Just do not forget to be well mannered and affordable, and you'll be surprised at how a good deal you can save. Who wants to be a pushover at the same time as you may be a confident negotiator?

Saving on Travel: Strategies for Cheap Flights, Accommodations, and Activities

In modern era-pushed worldwide, saving on adventure has come to be lots much less complex than ever. From finding cheap flights to coming across low-price accommodations and sports, there are some of tech-savvy techniques that tourists can use to maintain money. Here are a few guidelines on the manner to preserve on adventure using generation.

Use Flight Comparison Websites: One of the pleasant techniques to shop on air excursion is to apply flight assessment web

web sites which includes Kayak, Skyscanner, or Google Flights. These websites permit you to compare fees and flight instances during a couple of airways, and find out the best offers on airfare. Some even offer the selection to set up rate signs to inform you while costs drop.

Consider Alternative Accommodations: Hotels may be high priced, specifically in famous traveller destinations. Consider the usage of opportunity accommodations like tour rentals, hostels, or homestays, which can be an awful lot greater less expensive. Websites like Airbnb, HomeAway, or Hostelworld will let you discover low-cost and specific hotels that wholesome your finances.

Use Travel Apps: Travel apps like TripIt, Hopper, or Expedia will permit you to shop coins on adventure with the resource of offering deals and promotions on flights, resorts, and sports. Some apps even provide cash again rewards or loyalty points that you may redeem for future excursion.

Book Activities in Advance: Booking sports like excursions, excursions, or enchantment tickets in advance can help you hold coins on excursion. Websites like Viator or GetYourGuide offer a huge form of sports at discounted fees, and booking earlier will assist you to steady a gap and hold cash on the equal time.

Saving on excursion is much less complicated than ever manner to technology. By using flight contrast internet web sites, considering opportunity hotels, the use of tour apps, and booking sports in advance, visitors can shop extraordinary quantities of coins on their next adventure. With a piece little little bit of research and making plans, anybody can come to be a savvy traveller and revel in all the advantages of low-cost tour.

Join Loyalty Programs: Many airlines, lodges, and vehicle condominium businesses provide loyalty applications with a purpose to allow you to keep cash on future excursion. By turning into a member of those programs, you can earn elements or miles for every purchase, which can be redeemed without spending a dime flights, inn remains, or vehicle rentals. Some loyalty programs even provide elite fame, which comes with extra perks along with priority boarding or loose enhancements.

Be Flexible with Your Travel Dates: Being bendy along aspect your journey dates let you find out much less highly-priced flights and accommodations. Traveling within the direction of off-top times or on weekdays may be plenty more less high priced than journeying at some point of weekends or pinnacle season. Websites like Google Flights or Kayak provide flexible date search options that let you evaluate prices at some point of special journey dates.

Use Credit Card Rewards: Many credit score rating rating cards offer tour rewards applications that let you keep cash on journey. By the use of a adventure rewards credit card to your purchases, you could earn factors or miles that may be redeemed for flights, inn remains, or automobile leases. Some credit score rating score cards also provide more blessings which encompass travel insurance or airport lounge get right of entry to.

Book Connecting Flights: Direct flights can be greater handy, however they will be often more steeply-priced than connecting flights. By booking connecting flights, you can preserve a super amount of cash on airfare. Websites like Skyscanner or Kayak will will assist you to evaluate expenses for every direct and connecting flights, and will let you find the nice offers on airfare.

In summary, there are many tech-savvy techniques that travelers can use to maintain cash on journey. By the use of flight assessment web sites, thinking about alternative motels, using adventure apps, reserving sports activities sports in advance, becoming a member of loyalty programs, being bendy with excursion dates, using credit score rating card rewards, and reserving connecting flights, travelers can keep wonderful quantities of cash on their next adventure. With a chunk little little bit of making plans and research, everybody can grow to be a savvy tourist and revel in all of the benefits of less expensive adventure.

Planning a ride can be exciting, however it is able to moreover be highly-priced. Luckily, there are masses of techniques to keep on journey! Before booking your flights, try the use of evaluation net net websites like Skyscanner or Google Flights to find the extraordinary gives. You can also set up fee signals to get notified at the same time as charges drop. Who knows what great offers you would probable find out?

When it involves motels, bear in mind opportunity options like hostels or vacation rentals. Not best can they be a whole lot much less highly-priced than conventional hotels, but similarly they offer a very unique journey revel in. Plus, you would probable even make a few new friends alongside the way! Who desires to live in a boring lodge even as you could have an adventure?

Activities and sights can also upload up fast. Try seeking out unfastened or low-price options like museums, parks, and taking walks tours. Many cities furthermore provide discounted or free admission on awesome days of the week. And don't overlook to check for scholar or senior discounts if you're eligible! Who wants to pay complete rate at the equal time as you may explore for a bargain much less?

Another manner to keep on tour is to be flexible along side your dates and locations. If you're now not tied to a particular location or time-frame, you may be capable of discover inexpensive flights and hotels. It moreover may be a laugh to discover new places and step out of your comfort vicinity! Who wishes to paste to a rigid itinerary while you could go with the go together with the glide?

Finally, don't overlook to do your studies in advance than you skip. Look up local customs and etiquette, study a few easy terms in the community language, and discover if there are any hidden costs or prices you need to be aware about. Being informed and organized allow you to keep away from steeply-priced mistakes and revel in your journey to the fullest. Who wishes to be clueless even as you will be a savvy traveller?

Chapter 6: Investing For the Future

Investing is a essential step towards building wealth and securing a financially solid future. Whether you are virtually starting out or trying to develop your portfolio, there are numerous key strategies you could use to begin making an funding and building wealth.

Start with a Budget: The first step in the path of constructing wealth is to begin with a price range. By expertise your earnings and prices, you could create a plan to shop money and allocate charge range closer to making an investment. Start via setting a goal for a way an lousy lot you need to keep each month and recollect decreasing decrease again on pointless prices to loose up extra cash for making an investment.

Consider a Retirement Account: One of the most crucial investments you could make is in the path of your retirement. Consider putting in place a retirement account, along side a 401(excellent enough) or IRA, which help you to buy the destiny at the same time as furthermore supplying tax advantages. These bills will allow you to make a contribution pre-tax greenbacks, that can lower your taxable income and help you shop greater in the end.

Diversify Your Portfolio: A key approach for making an investment is to diversify your portfolio. By making an funding in pretty a few assets, along with stocks, bonds, and real assets, you could lessen your risk and probably earn better returns. Consider strolling with a monetary guide or using a robo-consultant provider to help you create a high-quality portfolio that aligns collectively with your funding goals.

Stay Disciplined and Patient: Investing for the future calls for challenge and staying power. It's crucial to stay dedicated to your funding plan and keep away from making impulsive picks primarily based on market fluctuations or brief-term income. Instead, popularity on long-term goals and paintings in the route of constructing a sturdy investment portfolio that might offer financial security for destiny years.

Investing is a crucial step in the course of constructing wealth and securing a financially sturdy destiny. By beginning with a fee range, considering a retirement account, diversifying your portfolio, and staying disciplined and affected man or woman, you may start making an investment and running closer to your monetary desires. Remember that making an investment is an extended-time period technique, and it requires commitment and place to acquire success. With the proper thoughts-set and method, everyone can start constructing wealth thru economic economic financial savings and investments.

Focus on Low-Cost Investments: Investing may be steeply-priced, especially almost about costs and commissions. To maximize your returns, don't forget focusing on low-fee investments, together with index charge variety or alternate-traded finances (ETFs), which have lower expenses and permit you to save money over time. These investments are also a exquisite manner to diversify your portfolio and reduce your risk.

Monitor Your Portfolio: It's vital to show your funding portfolio often to ensure that it remains aligned at the side of your investment desires. Review your portfolio periodically to decide if any changes need to be made, together with rebalancing your private home or selling underperforming investments. This will assist you stay at the right song toward your lengthy-time period investment goals.

Take Advantage of Tax Benefits: Many investments offer tax advantages that allow you to maintain coins in your tax invoice. For example, making an investment in a tax-advantaged retirement account, which encompass a 401(adequate) or IRA, will can help you lessen your taxable income and save money on taxes. It's essential to understand the tax implications of your investments and take advantage of any tax advantages available to you.

Educate Yourself: Investing may be complicated and hard, so it is crucial to teach yourself on the basics of making an investment and understand how one-of-a-kind funding products paintings. Consider analyzing books or taking on line guides to discover about making an funding, and are on the lookout for advice from monetary experts or relied on property. By coaching yourself and staying knowledgeable, you can make higher funding choices and collect your monetary dreams.

Investing for the destiny is a clever method for building wealth and securing a financially solid destiny. By focusing on low-price investments, monitoring your portfolio, taking advantage of tax benefits, and coaching yourself, you can start building a robust funding portfolio that aligns collectively in conjunction with your dreams. Remember that making an investment is a protracted-time period approach, and it requires difficulty, patience, and a dedication for your financial desires. With the right approach, absolutely everyone can start building wealth through economic financial savings and investments.

Are you prepared to start building your wealth? The first step is to installation a economic financial savings plan. Whether you're saving for a down rate on a house, a dream holiday, or your retirement, it's crucial to make saving a situation. Set a financial savings motive, make a price variety, and automate your monetary financial savings to make it clean and on hand. Who desires to be broke at the same time as you can be a saver?

Once you've built up a robust emergency fund, it's time to begin making an investment. Investing can appear intimidating, but it doesn't want to be. Start with the beneficial useful resource of teaching yourself on the fundamentals of making an investment and deciding on a low-rate index fund or ETF. Remember, time is your biggest asset in relation to investing, so begin early and stay disciplined. Who desires to be a economic expert while you can be a clever investor?

Another way to gather wealth is to attention on developing your income. This can also need to suggest negotiating a boost at artwork, beginning a factor hustle, or investing for your education or capabilities. The more money you are making, the more you could shop and invest. Who desires to accept plenty much less on the same time as you may motive for greater?

It's crucial to take into account that building wealth is a marathon, not a sprint. Stay targeted on your extended-term dreams, even when the quick-time period sacrifices may additionally feel tough. And don't get discouraged with the aid of setbacks or market downturns. Keep a groovy head and live the route. Who needs to give up while you could persevere?

As you start to see your economic savings and investments grow, it can be tempting to splurge on luxuries. But don't forget about to reward yourself in a manner that aligns together with your values and goals. Maybe you cope with yourself to a pleasant dinner or a present day tool, or probably you operate your wealth to offer once more in your community or manual a purpose you care approximately. Who needs to be selfish at the same time as you can be beneficiant?

Finally, recall that building wealth isn't pretty a lot the coins. It's about growing a existence of abundance and freedom. Focus on what topics most to you, whether or no longer that's spending time with cherished ones, pursuing your passions, or growing a exquisite impact inside the worldwide. Who desires to be trapped via economic stress at the same time as you could be empowered through manner of economic freedom?

Chapter 7: Living a Minimalist Lifestyle

Living a minimalist manner of life is about simplifying your existence and lowering the litter and chaos that could frequently accompany modern-day dwelling. By focusing at the matters that honestly rely and putting off the greater, you could experience numerous advantages that might reason a happier, more healthful, and further fulfilling lifestyles.

Reduced Stress: One of the most tremendous advantages of dwelling a minimalist way of life is decreased stress. By casting off the greater and simplifying your life, you may lessen the intellectual and physical muddle that would result in tension, melancholy, and extraordinary awful feelings. This will assist you to feel more relaxed, targeted, and content fabric, fundamental to a happier and more wholesome lifestyles.

Increased Productivity: Another benefit of dwelling a minimalist manner of lifestyles is elevated productivity. By simplifying your existence, you could attention at the topics that really depend and cast off the distractions and time-losing sports activities that can save you your productiveness. This will let you benefit your desires and make the maximum of a while and energy.

Financial Freedom: Living a minimalist way of lifestyles can also bring about monetary freedom. By decreasing your expenses and doing away with the greater, you could keep coins and invest within the subjects that certainly depend to you. This can bring about a greater gratifying life this is centered on reports and relationships, in preference to material possessions.

Environmental Benefits: Living a minimalist manner of existence can have super environmental blessings. By decreasing your consumption and waste, you could lessen your impact on the surroundings and promote sustainability. This allow you to stay a extra conscious and responsible life, while moreover contributing to a extra fit planet for future generations.

Living a minimalist life-style could have severa benefits that can purpose a happier, more wholesome, and more fascinating existence. By reducing stress, growing productiveness, carrying out economic freedom, and selling environmental sustainability, you may simplify your existence and attention at the matters that certainly depend. Whether you're honestly beginning out or on the lookout for to simplify your life, the benefits of a minimalist way of life are smooth, and that they'll will let you gain your dreams and live your excellent existence.

Improved Health: Living a minimalist manner of life also can have high superb results to your physical health. A cluttered and disorganized residing area can motive strain and anxiety, that can negatively impact your health. By simplifying your residing place, you may create a extra non violent and calming surroundings that may enhance your mental health and decrease pressure ranges. Additionally, having much less clutter ought to make it less difficult to maintain your living space clean and maintain actual hygiene, which could help save you ailments.

More Time: By eliminating the extra and focusing on the matters that sincerely count number, you could unfastened up extra time on your day for the activities and relationships which is probably maximum essential to you. Living a minimalist lifestyle will can help you keep away from the time-losing sports activities activities that could distract you out of your desires and values, allowing you to spend greater time at the matters that convey you pride and success.

Greater Self-Awareness: Simplifying your existence also can cause extra self-focus and a deeper information of your values and priorities. By doing away with the distractions and extra, you can interest on what virtually subjects to you, a good way to assist you to higher recognize your private alternatives, beliefs, and goals. This can purpose a extra amazing and actual existence that is aligned alongside facet your core values.

Increased Creativity: Finally, dwelling a minimalist way of life can also sell creativity and innovation. By simplifying your surroundings and decreasing distractions, you may popularity your power and interest in your modern interests. This can purpose new mind and upgrades, in addition to a extra enjoyable and amazing creative workout.

Living a minimalist manner of existence may want to have numerous blessings in your physical and highbrow fitness, your relationships, your finances, and your primary tremendous of lifestyles. By focusing on the topics that clearly depend and simplifying your life, you can benefit greater self-focus, advanced creativity, extra time, and advanced health, at the same time as additionally promoting environmental sustainability and social responsibility. Whether you are attempting to simplify your lifestyles or simply lessen the litter, the blessings of a minimalist way of life are easy, and that they will allow you to stay your brilliant life.

Living with tons less may be mainly releasing. When we simplify our lives, we free ourselves from the weight of greater stuff and commitments, and create location for what without a doubt subjects. Instead of being weighed down by using manner of possessions and responsibilities, we're able to interest on our relationships, our passions, and our personal boom. Who wishes to be overwhelmed at the same time as you could stay with clarity and purpose?

Simplifying our lives also can bring about more contentment and happiness. When we prevent chasing after material possessions and out of doors validation, we will locate pleasure in the easy pleasures of lifestyles. We can take delight in a outstanding e-book, a protracted walk, or a sizable conversation with a cherished one. Who wants to be constantly striving even as you'll be content cloth cloth with what you have got were given?

Living with masses much less can also have a first-rate effect on our surroundings. By ingesting a first-rate deal lots less and minimizing our waste, we are able to lessen our carbon footprint and help defend our planet. We can also assist sustainable practices and advise for guidelines that prioritize the fitness of our ecosystems. Who wants to damage the planet even as you can help defend it?

Simplifying our lives can also reason extra monetary stability and freedom. When we reduce our charges and stay internal our way, we're capable of store extra and work an entire lot an awful lot less. We moreover can be greater intentional with our spending and spend money on reviews and relationships that supply us right satisfaction and fulfillment. Who desires to be trapped with the resource of debt and overwork while you can live internal your method and prioritize what topics most?

Finally, simplifying our lives can result in greater peace and mindfulness. When we dispose of distractions and clutter, we create a area for quiet pondered photograph and inner stillness. We can domesticate a sense of gratitude and appreciation for what we've got, and discover peace within the present moment. Who needs to be burdened and tense at the same time as you could live with calm and mindfulness?

Chapter 8: What Is Frugalism And Why Is It Important?

Feudalism is a way of lifestyles that prioritizes spending an awful lot much less, saving more, and making practical economic alternatives. It is ready making the maximum of your property, whether or not it's some time, cash, or strength. Feudalism isn't approximately depriving yourself of the things you revel in or going without the necessities. Instead, it's far about locating innovative strategies to maintain cash and make your belongings stretch further.

The reasons why frugalism is critical can range from character to man or woman, but some not unusual reasons consist of trying to accumulate economic independence, decreasing debt, saving for retirement, or truely being capable of stay inner your manner. Frugal dwelling also can help you simplify your lifestyles, limit your effect on the surroundings, and reduce stress by using way of lowering the pressure to keep up with the Joneses.

Frugality is a mind-set that calls for subject, persistence, and a willingness to change your behavior. It calls with a purpose to keep in thoughts of your spending, to make informed picks, and to be willing to make sacrifices inside the brief-time period for lengthy-term income. By embracing frugalism, you may take control of your price range, reduce your prices, and enhance your traditional economic well-being.

Frugal dwelling is not just about reducing costs, it's far about making the maximum of what you have got. It calls with a purpose to be revolutionary, ingenious, and revolutionary. For example, as an opportunity of buying a brand new item, you can try repairing or repurposing a few detail you already very very own. Or in choice to consuming out, you may possibly strive cooking a meal at domestic the usage of substances you've got already were given reachable. These small changes can upload up through the years and make a huge effect to your budget.

In end, frugalism is a way of life that empowers you to take control of your price variety and gather your economic goals. Whether you're searching for to reduce debt, save for the destiny, or really stay indoors your manner, frugalism let you collect your desires and enhance your regular monetary well-being.

The Psychology of Frugality: Understanding Your Motivations

Frugality is not just about decreasing costs and saving cash; it's also approximately information the underlying motivations and feelings that stress our spending conduct. To really embody a frugal way of existence, it's far essential to understand the mental elements that affect our spending and increase techniques to overcome them.

One of the crucial issue mental factors which have an impact on our spending is the desire for fast gratification. We stay in a fast-paced worldwide wherein we need subjects now, and this choice can force us to make impulsive purchases. To counteract this, it is important to take a step decrease returned and recollect the extended-term consequences of our spending options. A frugal manner of life requires staying electricity and a willingness to watch for matters we want, in desire to shopping for them on a whim.

Another mental thing that impacts our spending is the choice to in shape in and be often happening by means of the usage of others. This can force us to make purchases that we might not constantly need or want, clearly because of the fact we want to preserve up with the Joneses. To triumph over this, it's far crucial to be confident in who you are and now not be swayed via the evaluations of others. Embrace the values and ideas which may be important to you, and do now not be afraid to transport in the direction of the norm.

Fear can also play a large function in our spending conduct. We might be afraid of strolling out of coins, or not having enough to cover our fees in the destiny. This worry can energy us to overspend in case you need to experience regular. To conquer this, it's miles essential to develop a robust monetary plan, bring together an emergency fund, and apprehend the significance of dwelling internal your method.

Finally, our feelings can also play a massive characteristic in our spending behavior. For instance, we would make purchases at the same time as we are feeling happy or all the way down to make ourselves revel in better. To counteract this, it's far essential to recognize the region that feelings play in our spending and enlarge techniques to govern them. For example, you'll probably take a stroll, meditate, or engage in each different interest that allows you manipulate your feelings in a wholesome manner.

In stop, the psychology of frugality is a complicated and multi-faceted issue be counted wide variety that requires a deep statistics of the motivations and emotions that force our spending conduct. By spotting the intellectual elements that have an impact on our spending and developing techniques to overcome them, we are capable of create a sustainable frugal lifestyle that permits us to take manipulate of our price variety and accumulate our economic goals.

Budgeting Basics: How to Create and Stick to a Budget

Budgeting is a critical detail of frugal residing and one of the keys to taking manipulate of your charge variety. A rate range is a monetary plan that lets in you understand your income and charges and provides a roadmap for attaining your monetary goals. By developing a price range, you can advantage clarity on your spending behavior, find out areas wherein you may cut fees, and prioritize your spending in a manner that aligns along with your values and goals.

Creating a price range can appear overwhelming, but it is simply a smooth system that anybody can do. The first step is to build up all of your monetary data, which embody your profits and costs. You can do this with the resource of reviewing your financial institution statements, pay stubs, and credit score card payments. This statistics will help you create an correct photograph of your budget.

Once you've got were given all of your monetary records, you could begin categorizing your costs. Common classes embody housing, transportation, food, amusement, and private care. You can use a spreadsheet or a budgeting app to help you hold song of your costs. It's important to be sincere and accurate at the same time as monitoring your charges, as this will help you are making knowledgeable choices about your spending.

After you have labeled your expenses, you may create a charge variety through subtracting your fees from your profits. This will provide you with a clean photo of your monthly surplus or deficit. If you have got were given a surplus, you can use it to repay debt, keep for the future, or invest in your economic future. If you have got were given a deficit, you could search for areas in which you could reduce costs or boom your income.

Sticking to a finances can be a assignment, however there are some strategies that would assist. First, it's miles important to be practical at the identical time as growing your price range. If you place unrealistic dreams, you will be much less likely to paste to them. It's furthermore essential to tune your spending regularly and regulate your fee variety as wanted. Finally, it is useful to have a system in place that lets in you live responsible and on route. This may encompass the usage of a budgeting app, running with a monetary consultant, or in reality speakme to a depended on pal or family member approximately your budgeting desires.

Budgeting is an crucial element of frugal dwelling in order to can help you take manage of your price range, reduce your costs, and reap your monetary dreams. By developing and sticking to a charge variety, you can create a sustainable financial plan that empowers you to stay a extra enjoyable and financially constant existence.

Reducing Your Housing Costs: Tips for Finding Affordable Housing

Housing is frequently one in all of the maximum crucial prices in a own family rate variety, so lowering your housing fees may also additionally have a huge effect for your economic well-being. Whether you are a renter or a residence owner, there are some of techniques you may use to lessen your housing costs and make your housing state of affairs greater low-value.

For renters, the first step in lowering your housing charges is to save round for the great deal. This would likely suggest seeking out condo houses that provide discounts for long-term rentals, or trying to find rental properties in areas with decrease rental fees. When searching out condominium homes, it is critical to endure in thoughts not simply the month-to-month hire, however moreover the fee of utilities, parking, and unique associated expenses.

Another method for decreasing housing expenses is to search for possibility housing options, together with shared housing or co-dwelling preparations. This may be an particularly appealing preference for single renters or those on a respectable charge variety, as shared housing often allows you to break up costs like hire and utilities with different renters.

For house owners, lowering housing prices can include making modifications to your house to make it more power-green. This ought to probably mean putting in insulation, upgrading your property domestic home windows, or putting in a programmable thermostat. These types of upgrades can lessen your monthly energy costs and enhance the overall comfort of your property.

Another strategy for reducing housing fees is to downsize to a smaller domestic. This might in all likelihood advocate selling your contemporary domestic and shifting to a smaller, more cheap home, or simply decluttering your cutting-edge home to make it more capability. Downsizing can be a excellent preference for retirees, empty-nesters, or anybody in search of to reduce their monthly fees.

In end, there are a number of strategies you may use to reduce your housing prices, whether or no longer you're a renter or a assets owner. By exploring your options and making changes in your housing situation, you could loose up extra of your monthly income for monetary savings and different monetary goals, and enhance your commonplace economic safety.

Frugal Food and Meal Planning: How to Save Money on Groceries

Food and grocery costs may be a massive portion of a family finances, but there are a number of techniques that let you lessen your meals prices and keep coins on groceries. From meal planning to buying at good deal grocery shops, those pointers can help you reduce your meals prices and improve your popular financial scenario.

The first step in lowering your meals costs is to create a meal plan for the week. This will help you recognize exactly what you need to shop for on the grocery maintain, and decrease the possibilities of overspending or impulse searching for. When planning your meals, make sure to endure in mind the nutritional desires of your own family, and search for recipes that use ingredients you have already were given to be had.

Another vital method for saving money on groceries is to use coupons and cut charge codes. Many grocery stores provide coupons and good deal codes via their internet websites and cellular apps, which you could use to store coins to your weekly grocery purchases.

Shopping at cut rate grocery shops additionally can be an powerful way to reduce your food prices. Discount shops provide a restricted choice of gadgets at decrease fees than traditional grocery shops. By shopping at those shops, you can shop cash in your groceries with out sacrificing excellent or variety.

In addition to buying at reduce fee stores, you may moreover reduce your meals fees with the aid of purchasing common or store-brand products. These merchandise are frequently clearly as true as their name-logo opposite numbers, however are priced significantly decrease. When seeking out popular products, make certain to observe fees and materials to make sure you are getting a good deal.

Another technique for lowering your meals prices is to buy in bulk. Buying gadgets like rice, beans, and pasta in bulk can save you coins ultimately, so long as you have were given had been given the storage area to shop the gadgets. If you do not have enough garage area at home, you could remember becoming a member of a bulk food co-op in your community, in which you can buy food in bulk with wonderful participants.

Finally, decreasing meals waste also can help you store cash on groceries. By planning your food, storing meals nicely, and the use of leftovers creatively, you can lessen the quantity of food you throw away and shop coins to your grocery invoice.

In conclusion, there are a number of techniques you may use to reduce your food prices and store cash on groceries. By meal making plans, the usage of coupons, shopping for at reduce charge shops, looking for popular merchandise, shopping for in bulk, and decreasing meals waste, you could lessen your meals charges and decorate your common economic state of affairs.

Chapter 9: How to Simplify Your Life and Save Money

Minimalism is a life-style preference that emphasizes living with lots tons much less and prioritizing critiques over possessions. By simplifying your existence and lowering muddle, minimalism allows you to hold cash, reduce strain, and growth your popular experience of happiness and contentment.

One of the primary benefits of minimalism is that it will let you keep cash. By proudly proudly proudly owning fewer possessions, you have got plenty less to keep and update, that may lessen your not unusual prices. Additionally, by using fending off impulse purchases and only looking for what you actually want, you may reduce your spending and enhance your financial state of affairs.

Another gain of minimalism is that it could assist reduce strain and increase your experience of happiness and contentment.

By owning fewer possessions, you have got got a good deal much less to smooth and preserve, that could unfastened up some time and strength for extra significant testimonies. Additionally, with the useful resource of focusing on studies in desire to material possessions, you can shift your focus far from the pressures of purchaser life-style and in the direction of what surely subjects to you.

To get began with minimalism, it's far important to begin via decluttering your own home. This can include sorting via your possessions and figuring out what to keep, sell, or donate. When decluttering, it's far important to be sincere with your self about what you in truth use and want, and what's simply taking up location in your property.

Once you have decluttered your property, it is essential to maintain training minimalist requirements in your every day existence. This can include averting impulse purchases, only looking for what you actually need, and choosing evaluations over possessions. Additionally, it is essential to maintain a minimalist mind-set and preserve to declutter your home as essential, so that you can preserve your lifestyles easy and free of muddle.

Another factor of minimalism is being mindful of your consumption. This can involve reducing your waste and being greater privy to the goods you buy and use. By decreasing your waste, you may moreover reduce your environmental impact and hold money with the aid of preserving off unnecessary purchases.

Minimalism let you maintain coins, lessen strain, and growth your ordinary experience of happiness and contentment. By decluttering your own home, working toward minimalist thoughts on your every day life, and being aware of your consumption, you could simplify your existence and enhance your financial state of affairs.

Energy Efficiency: How to Reduce Your Utility Bills

Energy ordinary performance is the practice of reducing your electricity consumption and decreasing your effect at the surroundings. By making small modifications in your property, you may reduce your energy utilization, decrease your software program bills, and improve your financial scenario.

One of the exceptional methods to reduce your energy usage is to enhance your home's insulation. This can incorporate including more insulation on your attic, sealing air leaks spherical your home windows and doors, and replacing vintage home home windows with greater electricity-green models.

Another manner to reduce your strength utilization is to improve your appliances and lighting fixtures. This can comprise replacing antique, inefficient domestic system with

Energy Star licensed fashions, using LED moderate bulbs as opposed to traditional incandescent bulbs, and using programmable thermostats to control your heating and cooling tool. By the usage of electricity-inexperienced home equipment and lights, you can reduce your strength usage and decrease your software application payments.

In addition to upgrading your home device and lighting, you could moreover reduce your power usage through way of being aware about your behavior. This can incorporate turning off lights and electronics even as you are not the use of them, putting your thermostat to an power-saving temperature, and taking short showers in location of baths.

It's additionally critical to remember of your strength utilization while purchasing new domestic tool and electronics. When trying to find new appliances, look for Energy Star licensed fashions, which can be designed to use much less power and reduce your effect on the surroundings. Additionally, preserve in mind shopping Energy Star licensed electronics, inclusive of televisions and laptop systems, which can be designed to be greater energy-inexperienced.

Finally, you could lessen your strength usage with the resource of taking part in energy conservation applications provided thru your software program program organization. These packages can contain reducing your energy utilization in some unspecified time in the future of top periods, using power-inexperienced home system, and participating in strength audits to end up privy to areas wherein you can enhance your power overall performance.

By making small adjustments in your home, being aware of your conduct, and taking part in strength conservation programs, you could reduce your power usage, lower your software payments, and improve your financial state of affairs. By adopting an electricity-efficient lifestyle, you may help guard the surroundings and decrease your effect in the international.

Shopping Smarter: Tips for Finding Deals and Avoiding Impulse Purchases

Shopping smarter is an important element of frugal residing. One of the fine strategies to maintain cash at the identical time as buying is to make a listing of what you need and preserve on with it. Before you purchase groceries, take some time to plot out your purchases and make a list of the objects you want. This will assist you avoid impulse purchases and maintain you focused on the gadgets you really need.

Another way to shop coins at the equal time as purchasing is to assess costs at super shops. This can incorporate checking on line stores, using rate assessment internet internet web sites, and travelling community shops to examine fees. By evaluating prices, you can discover the tremendous offers and keep money to your purchases.

In addition to evaluating expenses, you may moreover save coins with the aid of using coupons and taking benefit of income. This can include clipping coupons from your nearby newspaper or subscribing to coupon net websites, and checking your nearby stores for sales and clearance objects. By using coupons and taking benefit of income, you can keep cash in your purchases and enhance your financial state of affairs.

It's moreover critical to take into account of your behavior at the same time as buying. This can comprise warding off shopping whilst you're hungry, compelled, or tired, and keeping off shopping as a form of enjoyment. By being conscious of your behavior, you can lessen your impulse purchases.

Finally, you can store coins through looking for used devices as an opportunity of recent objects. This can contain shopping for at thrift shops, storage income, and on-line marketplaces, together with eBay. By looking for used devices, you may hold cash on your purchases, reduce your impact on the surroundings, and manual nearby corporations.

In quit, with the useful resource of way of making a listing, comparing costs, the use of coupons and taking benefit of sales, being aware of your conduct, and shopping for used gadgets, you may keep coins, enhance your monetary state of affairs, and decrease your effect on the surroundings. By looking for smarter, you may stay a greater frugal and sustainable life.

Investing in Your Future: How to Save Money for Retirement

Investing to your future is an vital detail of frugal dwelling. By saving coins for retirement, you could ensure a cushty and robust destiny for yourself and your loved ones.

One of the simplest processes to store cash for retirement is to begin early. The in advance you begin saving, the greater time your cash has to enlarge via compound hobby. This technique that the longer you hold, the more money you will have in retirement, even if you hold a smaller amount every month.

Another way to save coins for retirement is to take gain of retirement financial financial savings money owed. These debts are designed particularly for retirement financial savings and regularly provide tax benefits and agency enterprise organization matching contributions, if you want to will let you keep more money and increase your retirement monetary financial savings extra quick.

In addition to retirement economic economic savings payments, you can additionally shop cash for retirement through making an funding in stocks, bonds, and mutual price variety. By making an investment in a diverse portfolio, you can reduce your hazard and likely earn a higher pass again in your investment. However, it's miles important to go through in mind of your investment selections and are looking for the recommendation of a financial marketing representative if crucial.

Another manner to keep money for retirement is to stay underneath your approach. By decreasing your expenses and fending off debt, you may loose up extra cash every month to preserve in your destiny. This can involve cutting lower again on needless costs, along with consuming out and enjoyment, and prioritizing your spending on critical charges, together with housing, meals, and transportation.

Finally, you could keep coins for retirement with the useful useful resource of developing your income. This can incorporate taking over a element-time machine, starting a detail enterprise, or asking for a enhance at your current mission. By growing your income, you can hold more money and expand your retirement monetary financial savings greater speedy.

In cease, by way of way of starting early, taking benefit of retirement monetary financial savings money owed, making an funding in shares, bonds, and mutual rate variety, residing under your approach, and growing your earnings, you may save cash in your future and make certain a cushty and solid retirement.

Frugal Transportation: How to Save Money on Car Expenses and Alternative Transportation Options

Transportation is a large cost for plenty humans, however it would now not must be. By adopting a frugal thoughts-set, you may keep cash on your transportation charges and doubtlessly put off this rate altogether.

One of the handiest methods to keep cash on automobile fees is to maintain your automobile well. Regular preservation, which incorporates oil modifications and tire rotations, can increase the life of your car and decrease the need for steeply-priced safety. You can also shop cash on gas through the use of driving efficiently, such as accelerating and braking without issues and preserving off excessive-tempo using.

Another manner to keep cash on vehicle costs is to preserve in mind possibility transportation options, collectively with public transportation, carpooling, and cycling. By the usage of opportunity transportation, you could lessen the amount of time you spend the usage of and the quantity of coins you spend on gasoline, safety, and coverage.

In addition to possibility transportation, you may additionally preserve cash on car fees with the beneficial resource of buying a fuel-green vehicle. Hybrid and electric powered powered cars can extensively reduce your fuel charges and assist you store cash ultimately.

If you do want a vehicle, don't forget shopping for a used automobile in region of a contemporary one. Used cars are regularly loads an awful lot less steeply-priced than new cars and can nevertheless offer reliable transportation.

Finally, you can save coins on car prices via manner of being aware about your using conduct. This can encompass lowering the quantity of time you spend the use of and maintaining off pointless trips. You can also reduce your the usage of expenses through the use of carpooling, which also can assist reduce your carbon footprint.

In end, with the useful useful resource of preserving your car well, thinking about possibility transportation options, buying a gas-inexperienced car, buying a used automobile, and being aware of your the usage of conduct, you could shop coins for your transportation costs and potentially take away this fee altogether.

Health and Wellness on a Budget: How to Stay Healthy Without Breaking the Bank

Maintaining suitable fitness is vital, but it can also be pricey. By adopting a frugal thoughts-set, you may live healthy with out breaking the economic group.

One of the brilliant strategies to maintain your health is to devour a balanced food plan that consists of masses of fruits, greens, complete grains, and lean proteins. You can preserve coins on groceries by using the utilization of purchasing in-season produce, shopping for at good deal grocery shops, and meal making plans. Meal planning also will let you lessen food waste and avoid impulse purchases.

Another way to stay wholesome on a finances is to stay lively. Physical activity is vital for preserving appropriate health, and there are numerous low-charge or loose methods to live lively, at the side of walking, trekking, and cycling. You also may be part of a network sports activities enterprise or participate in institution fitness instructions for an extremely low rate.

In addition to bodily hobby, it's crucial to get sufficient sleep and manage strain. You can decorate your sleep with the useful aid of setting up a steady sleep schedule and developing a chilled sleep environment. You can manipulate strain with the aid of the use of training relaxation strategies, which include deep respiration and meditation, and appealing in sports which you revel in.

You can save cash on prescription drugs with the useful resource of comparing expenses at precise pharmacies and asking your physician if there are frequently going on alternatives in your medications.

Finally, it's important to have medical health insurance. If you're now not included through an business enterprise organization-sponsored fitness plan, don't forget shopping a low-charge medical health insurance plan through the health insurance marketplace.

In forestall, through ingesting a balanced eating regimen, staying energetic, getting enough sleep and handling pressure, considering opportunity options for medicinal capsules, and having health insurance, you can stay healthful without breaking the financial institution. By being frugal together together with your health and well being, you can live healthier and additional low priced lifestyles.

Chapter 10: How to Raise Children Frugally

Raising a family may be highly-priced, but it does now not must be. By adopting a frugal mind-set, you could offer your children with the exceptional viable existence at the same time as saving coins within the technique.

One of the best strategies to preserve cash as a family is to find out low-charge or loose sports activities to do together. This can encompass visiting parks and museums, taking element in network sports activities, and going on nature hikes. You also can keep cash on enjoyment through subscribing to streaming services in preference to cable TV, borrowing books and movies from the library, and growing your very personal amusing at domestic with arts and crafts factors.

When it comes to purchasing objects in your kids, recall buying used objects or hand-me-downs rather of recent items. This can encompass garb, toys, and little one equipment. You also can keep cash on college substances thru the utilization of purchasing income and shopping for everyday objects.

Another way to store cash as a family is to prioritize healthy consuming conduct. Cook food at home rather than eating out, and percentage your personal lunches for work and university. You can also hold coins on snacks with the useful resource of manner of buying in bulk and making your very very personal wholesome snacks, together with fruit and nut bars, at domestic.

It's also essential to teach your kids about the importance of saving cash. Encourage them to save their allowance and teach them the way to price range their cash. You can also teach them approximately the importance of giving decrease lower lower back through volunteering and donating to charity.

In stop, via finding low-charge or free activities to do together, purchasing used gadgets, prioritizing healthy ingesting behavior, and schooling your kids about the importance of saving coins, you may decorate your children frugally and offer them with the top notch viable life. By being frugal as a own family, you could construct a sturdy financial basis for the future.

Building an Emergency Fund: Why It's Important and How to Get Started

An emergency fund is a critical element of personal finance. It acts as a protection net in case of surprising sports along with task loss, clinical prices, or domestic protection. Without an emergency fund, you may come to be going into debt or dipping into your financial savings, that may have extended-time period financial results.

The first step in building an emergency fund is to decide your emergency fund intention. A cutting-edge guiding precept is to have three to 6 months of residing charges stored in case of a economic emergency. To calculate your residing fees, bear in mind all of your monthly charges, collectively with housing, meals, transportation, insurance, and other requirements.

Once you have were given were given determined your emergency fund purpose, it's time to begin saving. One of the awesome methods to keep for an emergency fund is to automate your monetary monetary savings. You can set up an immediate deposit out of your paycheck right proper into a separate monetary monetary financial savings account particularly to your emergency fund. This way, you can save while not having to maintain in mind it.

Another way to build your emergency fund is to search for approaches to reduce your monthly costs. This can include lowering decrease decrease returned on discretionary spending, along with ingesting out, amusement, and shopping for, and locating techniques to reduce your monthly bills, collectively with negotiating your cable or internet bill.

You can also undergo in thoughts growing your income via aspect hustles or requesting a enhance at paintings. Any more money you earn can be placed proper away into your emergency fund.

Building an emergency fund is critical for economic stability. By determining your emergency fund purpose, automating your monetary financial savings, lowering your month-to-month prices, and increasing your profits, you may assemble a sturdy emergency fund to guard your self and your circle of relatives in case of economic emergencies. Don't wait until it is too past due to start building your emergency fund - start in recent times!

Frugal Travel: How to Take Vacations Without Going into Debt

Travel is a superb way to relax, enjoy new cultures, and create memories that remaining an entire lifestyles. However, it may also be luxurious, and it is straightforward to turn out to be spending extra cash than you deliberate. If you want to take vacations without going into debt, it's miles vital to consider of your spending and undertake a frugal approach to tour.

One of the most important matters you may do to maintain coins on tour is to plot in advance. This approach learning your tour spot, finding gives on flights and motels, and setting a rate variety for your ride. It's also an top notch idea to examine charges for one in every of a type adventure dates to discover the excellent deals.

Another way to shop coins on tour is to search for opportunity lodges. Rather than staying in a motel, undergo in mind staying in a holiday apartment, hostel, or camping web page. This can save you cash on hotels and offer you with a very precise and immersive tour enjoy.

When it comes to meals, one of the terrific processes to shop cash is to cook dinner your personal meals. This can be completed thru manner of staying in a rental with a kitchen or by means of manner of the utilization of buying meals from neighborhood markets and cooking it yourself. Eating at close by consuming places also can be a amusing and budget-friendly manner to enjoy community cuisine.

It's critical to maintain in mind of transportation fees. This can encompass the fee of getting to and from your tour spot, further to transportation whilst you are there. Consider taking public transportation, strolling, or biking, in choice to renting a vehicle. If you do need to lease a car, have a look at expenses and remember automobile-sharing alternatives.

Another manner to hold cash on journey is to be aware about your amusement costs. Look for free of charge or low-rate activities, including traveling museums or hiking in close by parks. This will assist you to revel in your journey with out breaking the financial group.

Finally, it's far essential to have an emergency fund for tour. This will let you cover unexpected prices and make certain that your ride does no longer located you into debt.

Frugal excursion is all approximately being conscious of your spending and finding strategies to preserve coins at the same time as even though playing your revel in. With a bit little little bit of planning and steerage, you can take top notch vacations with out going into debt.

Do-it-yourself Projects: How to Save Money by way of the use of Fixing Things Yourself

DIY projects can be a amazing manner to store coins on the identical time as moreover analyzing new abilties and improving your private home or non-public objects. Whether you're solving a leaky tap, repairing a bit of furnishings, or building a bookshelf, taking on a DIY challenge can be a fun and budget-friendly interest. In this bankruptcy, we'll cover recommendations for efficiently finishing DIY duties and a way to make the maximum of your charge variety.

Getting Started:

Determine the scope of the mission: Before beginning any project, it's vital to apprehend what you're able to doing and what gadget and materials you'll need.

Research and gather facts: Look for tutorials or academic films online or are attempting to find advice from a how-to ebook.

Plan your budget: Determine the whole charge of the challenge, in conjunction with the rate of any essential equipment and materials.

Gather tool and substances: Consider shopping for 2nd-hand objects or the use of what you have already were given as an possibility of purchasing the whole lot new.

Working at the Project:

Work with a associate: Having a friend or member of the family paintings with you at the assignment may be useful, each in phrases of getting the activity carried out more fast and dividing the price of gear and substances.

Take it gradual: Rushing via a venture can lead to mistakes and mistakes may be expensive.

Follow safety precautions: Make positive to put on defensive tool and observe all protection measures to avoid damage.

Saving Money:

Use coupons and discounts: Check for income, coupons, and discounts at home development shops or on line.

Buy in bulk: If you're planning on taking over more than one obligations, looking for in bulk can save you cash in the end.

Reuse materials: Try to reuse materials or objects you have already got earlier than searching for new ones.

Compare charges: Take the time to assess costs of tools and substances at one-of-a-type shops to get the wonderful deal.

Chapter 11: How to Find Great Deals on Used Items

Secondhand purchasing is a extraordinary way to keep cash even as even though getting the belongings you want. Whether you are seeking out clothing, fixtures, electronics, or precise gadgets, there are numerous places to find lightly used gadgets at a fraction of the value of buying new.

One of the maximum popular places to find out secondhand objects is at thrift shops. Thrift shops regularly acquire donations from people, so the selection can be hit or omit, but you could regularly find superb gives on devices which may be in excellent condition. Look for thrift stores to your vicinity and make an addiction of stopping in often to look what's to be had.

Another notable area to find out secondhand devices is online. Websites like Craigslist and Face book Marketplace will permit you to search for items on your location and negotiate expenses with the seller straight away. These net web sites moreover have patron safety guidelines, so you can enjoy assured which you are growing a stable buy.

Garage profits and assets profits also are terrific locations to discover secondhand gadgets. Keep an eye constant on close by listings and be prepared to get up early on weekends to triumph over the crowds.

When looking for secondhand devices, it's crucial to investigate objects cautiously before creating a buy. Look for signs and signs and symptoms and signs and symptoms of damage and tear and tear and tear, and ask the vendor about the item's history and any recognized problems.

By incorporating secondhand searching for into your existence, you may maintain cash at the property you want even as decreasing your impact on the environment. With a touch patience and creativity, you can locate notable gives on lightly used objects and create a more frugal and sustainable manner of life.

Working from Home: How to Save Money on Commuting and Work-Related Expenses

Working from home has come to be increasingly more common in cutting-edge years, and it offers many blessings, at the side of the opportunity to keep money on commuting and paintings-related charges. By casting off the need to travel to and from the place of work, you could hold cash on fuel, public transportation, parking, and other commuting-related costs.

In addition to saving cash on commuting, running from home additionally will let you store cash on artwork-related fees. For instance, you can save cash on lunch with the resource of getting equipped your non-public meals, and you could additionally be able to save coins on apparel through not having to vicinity on industrial organization clothing every day.

To maximize your economic financial savings at the same time as working from home, it's crucial to have a devoted workspace that is separate from your residing location. This will assist you stay focused and efficient, and it's going to moreover let you declare a home place of business deduction on your taxes, that could similarly lessen your tax legal responsibility.

When working from domestic, it's furthermore important to have in thoughts of your energy usage. By turning off lighting fixtures and electronics while now not in use, you may reduce your energy invoice and assist the environment.

In addition to saving money, running from home also can offer extra flexibility and manage over your schedule. With the potential to artwork from everywhere with a web connection, you can spend extra time with family and friends, journey more, and experience a better artwork-life stability.

By embracing the blessings of working from domestic, you may benefit a more frugal and sustainable way of life. With a hint making plans and strive, you may keep coins on commuting and art work-related prices on the identical time as playing the liberty and flexibility of operating from domestic.

Freelancing: How to earn greater earnings from detail hustles

Freelancing is a famous manner for human beings to supplement their earnings and create a bendy paintings time table. With the upward push of the gig monetary device, it has by no means been easier to reveal your talents and passions proper proper right into a profitable aspect hustle. Whether you are an artist, author, developer, or marketer, there are endless opportunities to offer your services as a freelancer.

Here are some suggestions for beginning and growing a a fulfillment freelancing business business enterprise:

1.   Identify your vicinity of hobby: Think approximately what talents you have got were given had been given that would be in name for and research the interest market to look what styles of freelance artwork are available.

2.   Build your portfolio: Create a portfolio that showcases your work and highlights your know-how. This is probably crucial even as attaining out to ability customers and bidding on tasks.

3.   Network: Join on-line corporations, attend occasions, and connect with one-of-a-kind freelancers to assemble your community and find new opportunities.

four. Set your expenses: Research market rates to your area of interest and determine a rate that as it need to be displays your enjoy and expertise diploma. Be confident to your pricing and be inclined to negotiate at the same time as essential.

five. Market yourself: Promote your services on social media, your non-public net website on line, and special structures. Consider accomplishing out to capacity clients right now and supplying your offerings.

6. Manage your finances: Make sure to hold song of your income and fees, set apart cash for taxes, and take into account making an investment in system that assist you to manipulate your company efficiently.

7. Stay organized: Keep tune of cut-off dates, invoices, and challenge records so that you can live on top of your work and supply fantastic results.

By following those hints, you could turn your freelance enterprise business enterprise right right into a a hit and worthwhile challenge. Whether you are searching for to complement your profits or pursue a full-time profession as a freelancer, it is never too beyond due to start.

Growing your personal meals: How to save coins on groceries thru developing your non-public produce

Growing your non-public food is a notable way to keep coins on groceries and devour more healthy. By growing your non-public stop end result and greens, you've got control over the first-class of the food you eat, and you could moreover lessen your carbon footprint with the useful resource of lowering the space your meals has to journey. There are many one-of-a-kind strategies to begin growing your non-public meals, whether you have a huge backyard or exceptional a small balcony.

1.   Choose the proper vicinity: Make fine the vicinity you select has get right of entry to to daytime and is covered from wind and different harsh climate situations. Consider elements collectively with soil kind, water

availability, and what kind of area you have to be had.

2.   Choose the right plant life: Choose plants which are nicely-perfect on your developing conditions and weather. Consider the quantity of area, sun publicity, and soil kind at the same time as choosing flora. Also, pick out flowers that you and your circle of relatives need to consume, this may make it much less complex to use the produce you expand.

3.   Start small: If you are new to gardening, begin with some clean-to-broaden vegetation like herbs, tomatoes, or lettuce. As you benefit experience, you could add greater flora on your garden.

four. Use bins: If you don't have loads region or soil, undergo in thoughts using containers. Containers can be made of different substances, which consist of plastic, clay, or timber, and can be located on balconies, patios, or windowsills.

5.   Use herbal techniques: Avoid using chemical materials and insecticides in your lawn, and instead use natural techniques to manipulate pests and illnesses. This will make your food greater regular to eat, and furthermore allows the environment.

6.   Plan ahead: Make a plan for the manner you may use the produce you increase, so you can make sure that you're planting the right amount of each plant. Plan to hold some of your produce to be used sooner or later of the wintry climate months.

By growing your personal meals, you may shop coins on groceries, eat more healthy, and decrease your carbon footprint. It's moreover a great manner to spend time outdoor, get some exercising, and hook up with nature. Whether you have got have been given a huge outdoor or only a small balcony, there may be a way on the way to start developing your very own food.

Retirement Planning: How to Save Money for the Future and Enjoy Retirement

Retirement planning is a vital element of financial planning that enables people make certain a snug and secure retirement. The motive of this financial disaster is to help you recognize the significance of retirement planning and a way to save coins for the destiny so you can revel in your retirement years.

Chapter 12: Why Is Retirement Planning Crucial?

Retirement making plans is critical as it allows people put together for the financial realities of retirement. The rate of residing wills growth over the years, and those need to have enough monetary savings to preserve their full-size of residing in retirement.

How to preserve cash for retirement?

1.   Start early: The earlier you start saving for retirement, the more time your financial monetary financial savings ought to develop. The power of compounding interest manner that your financial monetary financial savings can expand exponentially over the years, so beginning early can also have a wonderful effect to your retirement economic financial savings.

2.   Create a price range: Create a price range that consists of saving for retirement. Determine how an entire lot you could find

the money for to maintain every month and make sure to paste for your charge variety.

three. Contribute to a retirement plan: Consider contributing to a retirement plan. Many employers provide matching contributions, because of this that you may hold more for retirement through contributing for your plan.

four. Invest wisely: Invest your retirement economic financial financial savings in a various portfolio of low-rate mutual charge range or index budget. This assist you to acquire better returns and restrict your hazard.

five. Consider extraordinary savings automobiles: Consider other financial economic financial savings vehicles, together with annuities or lifestyles coverage rules, to help you hold for retirement.

6. Live under your method: To save more for retirement, you want to stay

underneath your way. This approach spending plenty much less than you earn and keeping off debt as an awful lot as possible.

7. Plan for prolonged-term care: Long-term care charges may be large in retirement, so it's far crucial to plot for them. Consider buying extended-term care coverage or saving for lengthy-term care in a completely unique account.

Enjoying retirement

Retirement may be an interesting time, but it can additionally be worrying in case you do not have enough economic monetary savings to aid your self. By saving cash for the destiny and making plans for retirement, you can make sure which you have the financial safety you want to experience your retirement years. Consider what you want to do in retirement, together with tour, spend time with family, or pursue interests, and make sure you have were given sufficient monetary monetary savings to assist the ones sports.

In give up, retirement planning is a important element of financial making plans. By beginning early, growing a finances, contributing to a retirement plan, making an funding appropriately, and living under your method, you can store cash for the destiny and experience a comfortable and strong retirement.

Debt Reduction: How to Pay Off Debt and Improve Your Financial Situation

Debt can be a heavy burden and effect your normal monetary balance. Whether it's from credit score rating cards, scholar loans, or private loans, the purpose of debt discount is to pay it off as short as feasible at the equal time as minimizing hobby expenses.

Here are some steps to help you lessen your debt:

1.   Assess Your Debt: Make a listing of all your debts, together with the creditor, hobby rate, and minimum rate due. This will come up with a clean photograph of your monetary state of affairs and assist you prioritize which debts to repay first.

2.   Create a Budget: Creating a budget is a important step in lowering debt. This will help you allocate funds to pay off your money owed on the identical time as despite the fact that buying vital fees.

three. Prioritize Your Debts: Pay off high-hobby debt first, as it will fee you greater in the long run. Consider the use of the debt snowball or debt avalanche approach to prioritize your debt reimbursement.

4.   Increase Your Income: Look for tactics to increase your profits, which includes freelancing, issue hustles, or soliciting for a enhance. The greater income may be used to pay off debt quicker.

five. Cut Expenses: Reducing fees is any other way to unfastened up cash to pay off debt. Look for techniques to maintain coins in your budget, which embody cutting once more on ingesting out or decreasing your grocery invoice.

6. Make Extra Payments: Make extra payments to repay debt quicker and maintain on interest charges.

7. Avoid Accruing More Debt: Once you start paying off debt, it's vital to avoid accruing more debt. Avoid using credit score score cards and removing loans till it's essential.

Debt bargain requires issue and patience, but the cease cease result is properly well worth it. By paying off debt, you could decorate your monetary state of affairs and feature peace of mind information that you're debt-unfastened.

Insurance: How to discover the right coverage and store cash on expenses

Insurance is a important a part of private finance and protecting your property, but it is able to additionally be taken into consideration one in each of the most important costs to your finances. However, via way of data the outstanding types of insurance, evaluating guidelines, and buying spherical, you can find out the proper insurance and store money on your expenses.

The first step to finding the right insurance coverage is to apprehend your goals. This may encompass medical insurance, lifestyles coverage, vehicle insurance, house proprietors or renters insurance, and crook duty coverage. By taking an inventory of your property, liabilities, and destiny plans, you may determine which varieties of coverage you want and what form of coverage you want to have.

Once you've got were given a smooth facts of your insurance needs, it's time to begin comparing recommendations. Make sure to don't forget elements which encompass the insurance amounts, deductibles, and the recognition of the coverage company. It's moreover critical to have a look at the fine print and understand the exclusions, obstacles, and the technique for filing claims.

One of the nice techniques to keep cash on coverage charges is to hold spherical. Get prices from a couple of coverage companies and study their offerings. Don't be afraid to negotiate, as coverage companies often have room to decrease their rates to win your commercial enterprise organization.

Another way to save coins on insurance is to package deal your policies. Many insurance companies provide reductions for customers who've a couple of tips with them. For example, when you have each your vehicle and residence owners coverage with the same organisation business agency, you will be eligible for a reduction.

Finally, it's crucial to regularly evaluate your coverage coverage to make certain it maintains to meet your desires. Life sports, consisting of having married, having children, or searching for a cutting-edge domestic, can all impact your coverage dreams, and it's crucial to make sure your insurance is updated to reflect the ones modifications.

By following these guidelines, you may discover the right insurance insurance and keep cash on your costs. Protecting your property and securing your destiny is critical, and with a chunk strive and studies, you may achieve this on the same time as maintaining your charge variety in take a look at.

Estate Planning: How to Protect Your Assets and Plan for the Future

Estate making plans is a critical element of a complete economic plan. It includes organizing your property and liabilities, making choices approximately your destiny, and making preparations for the distribution of your house after loss of existence. This monetary catastrophe will assist you apprehend the importance of assets planning and provide tips on the way to protect your property and plan for the future.

Why is property making plans vital?

Estate making plans is vital for numerous motives. It enables make sure that your needs are determined, your assets are blanketed, and your family are looked after after your death.

What have to be included in an estate plan?

An belongings plan want to embody a will, believe, power of prison expert, and boom fitness care directive. A will is a crook record that outlines the manner you need your property to be distributed after your lack of existence. A take shipping of as actual with is a prison arrangement that permits you to preserve and control belongings for the advantage of someone else. Strength of prison expert gives a person else the authority to behave to your behalf in case you becomes incapacitated. An enhance fitness care directive outlines your needs concerning medical remedy in case you come to be no longer capable of make choices for yourself.

How you are capable of shield your property?

There are numerous procedures to shield your house, which embody developing a residing bear in mind, shopping for insurance, and gifting assets. A dwelling bear in mind permits you to interchange ownership of your house to a trustee at the equal time as you are notwithstanding the fact that alive. This can assist lessen the tax burden on your house and decrease the fees associated with probate court docket court docket instances. Insurance can offer monetary protection on your family in the occasion of your death. Gifting assets can assist lessen the size of your home, making it less complicated to manipulate and decreasing the tax burden in your property.

In end, property planning is an vital difficulty of a entire monetary plan. It lets in make certain that your desires are accompanied, your home are covered, and your own family are taken care of after your lack of lifestyles. By which include a will, believe, strength of felony expert, and increase fitness care directive on your private home plan, you may take manipulate of your financial future and protect your private home.

Tax Planning: How to shop coins on taxes and take gain of tax breaks

One of the critical aspect factors of frugal dwelling is maximizing your income and minimizing your expenses. This includes taking benefit of all the tax breaks and deductions you are eligible for. By understanding the tax code and planning your fee range as a quit result, you could appreciably lessen your tax invoice and maintain more of your difficult-earned cash.

Here are a few pointers for effective tax making plans:

1.   Keep accurate information: To claim all of the deductions and credit you are entitled to, it's miles important to keep accurate data of your income and fees. This includes receipts, payments, and financial group statements.

2.   Understand the one of a type sorts of taxes: There are numerous forms of taxes, which includes profits tax, earnings tax, belongings tax, and others. Understanding the awesome kinds of taxes will help you perceive the deductions and credit that look at to you.

three. Take gain of deductions: There are many deductions available, which consist of those for loan interest, charitable donations, and clinical costs. By taking benefit of these deductions, you may considerably lessen your taxable earnings.

four. Consider tax credits: Tax credit rating are even extra precious than deductions due to the reality they lessen your tax invoice greenback for dollar. For instance, the Earned Income Tax Credit offers a awesome tax credit score to low-profits taxpayers.

5. Plan for retirement: Retirement debts offer tax benefits, in conjunction with deductions for contributions and tax-unfastened growth of your investments. By contributing to the ones debts, you could reduce your taxable income and prepare for a stable economic destiny.

6. Seek expert recommendation: Tax criminal hints are complicated and trade often. By searching out the advice of a tax expert, you can make certain which you're taking gain of all the deductions and credit score score available to you.

By following the ones guidelines, you can efficiently control your taxes and keep extra of your hard-earned coins. Remember, tax planning is an ongoing gadget that requires regular interest to detail and an extensive information of the tax code.

Chapter 13: How to Save Money thru Shopping Online

Online purchasing has emerge as an more and more famous manner to shop for gadgets and services, supplying clients with comfort and a huge preference of merchandise at their fingertips. Not only is it a lot much less complicated to assess expenses and discover reductions, but buying online additionally presents an possibility to keep cash. In this bankruptcy, we can explore the best techniques to maintain cash on the equal time as buying on line.

1.   Use Coupon Codes: One of the best methods to preserve coins at the same time as buying on line is to use coupon codes. Many online shops offer specific discounts for customers who use a promo code in the course of checkout. You can discover those codes through doing a quick are searching for on Google or at the store's internet site. Some shops moreover provide electronic

mail or mobile notifications for specific earnings and reductions.

2. Comparison Shop: Another manner to hold money even as shopping for online is to assess fees on multiple internet websites. With some clicks, you can without problems evaluate expenses on exclusive internet web sites to make certain you are getting the first-class deal.

three. Shop During Sales: Many online shops provide earnings and unique promotions in the course of the one 12 months, so maintain a be careful for those. Some internet web sites actually have a committed segment for clearance gadgets, wherein you may discover superb offers on products which may be being phased out.

four. Use Cashback Sites: Cashback web websites provide clients a percentage in their buy charge lower lower back inside the form of cashback. When you keep through a cashback internet net web page, you can earn a advantageous percent lower again to your buy, which can be redeemed for coins or as a credit score rating rating within the direction of future purchases.

5. Take Advantage of Free Shipping: Shipping fees can add up speedy, specifically whilst looking for more than one devices. To store coins, look for stores that provide unfastened transport, or be part of up for a loose trial of a delivery software like Amazon Prime. Some stores moreover offer loose shipping for orders over a exceptional amount, so remember consolidating your purchases to take benefit of this offer.

6. Use Price Tracking Tools: Price tracking system let you track the rate of a selected object through the years and notify you even as the fee drops. This is specially beneficial for huge-price tag gadgets or for those who've a difficult and rapid budget for a specific object.

7.   Look for Refurbished or Used Items: Shopping for refurbished or used gadgets may be a first rate manner to store cash on the identical time as shopping for on-line. You can regularly locate tremendous offers on gently used objects, and refurbished objects are regularly actually as accurate as new, however at a decrease fee.

Shopping on-line may be a high-quality way to save coins, mainly in case you take advantage of the severa coins-saving pointers cited above. By the use of reductions, evaluation purchasing, buying at some point of income, the use of cashback web sites, taking benefit of unfastened delivery, using fee tracking gadget, and looking for refurbished or used devices, you can revel in the gain of on-line purchasing for at the identical time as moreover saving coins.

Saving coins on pursuits: How to experience your pursuits without spending too much

Hobbies are a brilliant manner to spend your entertainment time, but they can also upload up quick. From looking for new gadget to buying commands or sports, interests can brief drain your monetary institution account. However, with a piece creativity and making plans, you could despite the fact that enjoy your pastimes without breaking the financial organization. Here are some hints for saving money in your hobbies:

Prioritize your pursuits:

Start through considering which pursuits you revel in the most and which of them you could do with out. By focusing at the interests you want the maximum, you can maintain cash via manner of warding off those you don't experience as an awful lot.

Get innovative:

Think about opportunity techniques to engage on your hobbies. For example, if you love photos, as an alternative of purchasing a new digital camera, try the usage of your smartphone camera or borrow a digital camera from a pal. You can also strive running closer to your images competencies for your community park alternatively of purchasing a experience to a scenic location.

Look free of charge or low-rate alternatives:

Many towns provide loose or low-fee training, workshops, and activities for plenty of pastimes. Check your neighborhood network center or library for records on instructions or activities for your location.

Buy used or refurbished machine:

If you want to shop for device to your hobby, look for used or refurbished options. Sites like eBay, Craigslist, and Facebook Marketplace offer used items at a fraction of the fee of new device.

Join a club or institution:

Joining a membership or institution targeted round your interest may be a outstanding way to save cash. By sharing assets, inclusive of device and substances, you can preserve coins on the costs of your interest.

Trade abilities:

Consider buying and selling abilties with others who have complementary pastimes. For instance, in case you're into gardening, change talents with a person who's into woodworking. This way, you may keep cash on tool and property through sharing assets.

Plan in advance:

Planning ahead permit you to store coins on your pastimes. By setting a price range, you can keep away from overspending on device and supplies. Planning ahead can also help you find gives and promotions on the gadgets you want to your interest.

By following those tips, you could hold to enjoy your pursuits without putting too much strain in your budget. With a bit creativity and planning, you can save coins and still have amusing collectively together with your pastimes.

Money-saving apps: How to use generation to save cash

Technology has revolutionized many factors of our lives, which include our budget. With such an entire lot of cash-saving apps to be had, it is much less tough than ever to take control of your spending and start saving cash. In this economic catastrophe, we can find out some of the maximum famous cash-saving apps and how you may use them to reap your economic desires.

1.   Budgeting apps

Budgeting apps are designed that will help you music your spending and create a rate range that works for you. Those apps hyperlink in your monetary group debts and credit gambling cards, automatically categorizing your spending and imparting you with a smooth picture of your income and charges. With this records, you could create a charge variety that lets in you to maintain extra cash and reduce your spending in regions in which you'll be overspending.

2.   Cashback and rewards apps

Cashback and rewards apps provide you the possibility to earn coins lower back to your purchases by using means of purchasing via their app. Those apps also provide precise gives and promotions, making it even less complex to keep coins for your purchases.

3.   Coupon apps

Coupon apps assist you to save cash through manner of finding discounts and promotions in your selected services and products. Simply look for the products or services you are interested by, and the app will provide you with a listing of to be had coupons and promo codes. This can be a high-quality manner to shop cash on ordinary purchases like groceries, apparel, and amusement.

four. Investment apps

Investment apps allow you to invest small amounts of cash in a whole lot of stocks, bonds, and exceptional investment alternatives. Those apps provide instructional assets and device that will help you make informed funding alternatives, so that you can increase your wealth through the years.

five. Money transfer apps

Money transfer apps can help you fast and with out issues deliver cash to buddies and own family. Apps like Venmo, PayPal, and Cash App make it clean to ship cash, and some even provide on the spot transfers. This can be a convenient and cost-powerful manner to ship coins, specially in case you want to supply cash fast.

There are many cash-saving apps to be had to help you reach your monetary goals. Whether you are looking for to create a charge variety, earn cashback to your purchases, discover reductions, invest your cash, or ship cash to pals and own family, there may be an app for that. By incorporating these apps into your economic ordinary, you could take manipulate of your spending and begin saving cash nowadays.

Staying Committed to Frugality: How to Maintain Your Frugal Lifestyle Over Time

Adopting a frugal way of life may be a project, specifically if you're used to spending cash freely. However, the blessings of living frugally - saving cash, reducing debt, and developing financial safety - take the time nicely genuinely well worth it. In this bankruptcy, we are going to discover some recommendations for staying devoted to a frugal manner of existence and averting not unusual pitfalls.

Set desires and music development:

Setting easy financial goals is a key part of preserving a frugal way of life. Write down your dreams, whether or not or not it is paying off debt, saving for a down fee on a residence, or without a doubt building up your emergency fund. Keeping music of your improvement is also crucial. For example, you can create a fee variety spreadsheet, preserve a spending diary, or use a budgeting app to reveal your spending and financial monetary financial savings.

Stay prepared:

Organizing your budget is a crucial part of preserving a frugal way of lifestyles. Keep song of your payments and due dates, create a budget and stick with it, and use generation to help you keep coins and avoid overspending. Apps can help you stay organized and on the right tune.

Avoid impulse purchases:

Impulse purchases can be a massive drain for your price variety, in particular if you're looking for to maintain a frugal manner of life. To keep away from impulse purchases, try and hold on with a buying listing, keep away from browsing the mall or on-line buying web web sites even as you're bored or burdened, and keep in mind a 24-hour ready duration earlier than making any massive purchases.

Use coupons and earnings:

Using coupons and taking gain of sales will let you keep coins on groceries, clothing, and special regular costs. You can find coupons for your community newspaper, on line, or thru buying apps. When buying on line, make an effort to evaluate expenses and look for discounts or promo codes.

Shop secondhand:

Shopping secondhand may be a excellent way to store coins and decrease waste. Consider buying at thrift stores, storage income, and on line marketplaces like eBay and Facebook Marketplace for gently used garb, furniture, and family gadgets.

Re-examine your prices regularly:

It's essential to regularly re-have a look at your charges to appearance in case you're spending an excessive amount of cash in any man or woman location. For instance, if you're spending numerous coins on ingesting out, recall cooking more food at home, or in case you're spending plenty on amusement, endure in thoughts finding unfastened or low-price alternatives.

Stay stimulated:

Staying stimulated can be a mission, in particular whilst you're making big adjustments in your spending conduct. Surround yourself with supportive pals and own family, praise your self at the same time as you acquire your economic goals, and do no longer be too tough on yourself if you slip up. Remember that frugality is a journey, not a destination, and that small adjustments can upload as masses as big monetary savings over the years.

Find frugal alternatives in your preferred sports activities sports:

Living frugally does now not advise giving up all the matters you want. Instead, locate frugal options to your favorite sports, which incorporates trekking in choice to going to the films, or internet website hosting potluck dinners rather than eating out.

Living frugally takes strive, but the rewards - each monetary and personal - make it truly well really worth it. By putting desires, staying prepared, keeping off impulse purchases, buying secondhand, re-evaluating your charges, staying stimulated, and locating frugal options, you can maintain a frugal manner of existence and gain economic protection through the years.

Chapter 14: The Unexpected Discovery

For as long as I must keep in mind, I had been chasing the subsequent large purchase. It started with toys as a little one, after which advanced to greater highly-priced gadgets as I were given older. I grow to be generally looking for the current system, the modern style trend, the flashiest vehicle. It wasn't until my mid-twenties that I stumbled upon a sudden discovery that modified my existence all of the time.

It occurred on an afternoon similar to any other. I became surfing thru my social media feed, scrolling thru pictures of my pals' modern-day purchases, as soon as I got here across a placed up that caught my eye. It became a photograph of a girl sitting in a minimalist dwelling room, surrounded by means of manner of using just a few carefully curated gadgets. The caption take a look at, "Living a frugal lifestyles has brought me more pleasure than any material ownership ever need to."

I have become intrigued. Up till that thing, I had in no manner taken into consideration the possibility that living a frugal lifestyle need to deliver happiness. I clicked on the girl's profile and commenced to examine her tale. She had as quickly as been a massive spender, just like me. But she had found that constantly chasing after cloth possessions had left her feeling empty and unfulfilled.

As I continued to study, I commenced to realize that the severa matters that had brought me transient pleasure inside the beyond had in the end left me feeling the same manner. I remembered the satisfaction I felt as soon as I sold a brand new cellular phone, only to enjoy bored with it some weeks later. I concept approximately the instances I had lengthy past on extravagant vacations, satisfactory to go back again back feeling greater careworn than ever.

I changed into all of sudden overcome with a choice to take a look at more about this frugal way of existence. I started out out doing studies, studying blogs and searching movies about the way to live a less difficult, extra intentional existence. I found out approximately budgeting and meal making plans, and I commenced to peer how small adjustments must add as a lot as large financial savings.

At first, the concept of cutting again on my spending made me experience stressful. I modified into afraid that I may want to no longer be capable of preserve my way of life, that I could probable should surrender the topics that I loved. But as I started to region into effect some of the guidelines I had found out, I started to sense a feel of freedom that I had in no manner expert in advance than.

I started out to locate pleasure inside the easy subjects, like cooking a meal from scratch or going for a walk in the park. I started to realize the gadgets I already owned, in location of continuously feeling the want to shop for more. I even started to enjoy the machine of saving cash, looking my economic institution account develop with each passing month.

Now, years later, I appearance returned on that sudden discovery due to the fact the turning detail in my existence. It become the on the spot that I located out that actual happiness isn't positioned in fabric possessions, but inside the relationships we cultivate and the memories we have. I though have moments as soon as I slip again into vintage conduct, but I constantly come lower decrease returned to the education I determined out at some point of that transformative time.

The frugal manner of lifestyles is not for every person, however for me, it's been a supply of extraordinary delight and achievement. I am thankful for that sudden discovery, and for the opportunity to live a far less complicated, greater intentional lifestyles.

Learning the Basics of Frugalism

As I delved deeper into the world of frugalism, I fast decided out that there has been masses to examine. I had generally concept of myself as a reasonably thrifty character, but I had in no manner surely understood the energy of frugal dwelling till I started out out out to discover it in earnest.

The first detail I observed changed into that budgeting is the cornerstone of a frugal manner of lifestyles. I had commonly had a brand new concept of the way a good buy I spent every month, but I had in no way created an extensive rate range that accounted for all of my prices. When I sat right all of the manner right down to do that for the primary time, I became bowled over to appearance how an lousy lot I became spending on such things as eating out and shopping for.

Creating a budget compelled me to confront a few uncomfortable truths about my spending behavior. I decided out that I come to be using my credit rating card more than I must, and that I became frequently making impulse purchases without wondering via the results. But at the same time, I felt empowered by means of the facts that I now had the equipment to take control of my charge range.

The subsequent element I located became the importance of meal making plans. Before I began residing a frugal way of existence, I might regularly go to the grocery keep with out a plan and grow to be shopping for extra than I wanted. I ought to then allow meals visit waste due to the truth I did not have a plan for the way to use it.

Now, I create a weekly meal plan and purchasing listing earlier than I visit the store. This not best enables me maintain cash through using the usage of purchasing handiest what I need, but it moreover permits me avoid the temptation to consume out due to the fact I actually have a plan for what I will devour at domestic.

Another essential detail of frugal living is finding methods to reduce waste. This can recommend some element from composting food scraps to the usage of reusable buying bags. One of my non-public examples of this have become after I began out the use of a reusable water bottle as an alternative of purchasing disposable plastic bottles. This no longer fantastic saved me cash, but it furthermore helped lessen my impact at the surroundings.

Frugalism additionally taught me the fee of taking care of what I already owned. Instead of constantly seeking out new garments, I commenced out mending and repurposing those I already had. I moreover commenced taking higher care of my possessions, whether or not it became thru often cleaning my automobile or getting my footwear resoled as an opportunity of purchasing new ones.

All of those small adjustments added as much as massive financial savings over the years. But more importantly, they helped me stay a more intentional and satisfying existence. I no longer felt like I modified into constantly chasing after the subsequent massive buy, however as an opportunity end up content material cloth fabric with what I had.

Learning the fundamentals of frugalism turned into no longer continuously smooth. It required me to confront a few uncomfortable truths about my spending conduct and make some huge changes in my lifestyles. But the advantages were extra than definitely definitely worth it. I now experience extra on top of factors of my rate range, and I certainly have a deeper appreciation for the things that in fact matter range in life.

The Joy of Living with Less

As I endured to embody frugalism, I positioned a few aspect surprising: the pleasure of living with less. In a society that frequently equates cloth possessions with success and happiness, it may be hard to anticipate that having a great deal much less must simply cause a extra eye-catching life. But this is precisely what I determined to be actual.

One of the primary subjects I did as soon as I started out out living extra frugally was to declutter my home. I had constantly been a chunk of a packrat, maintaining onto matters I didn't really need "surely in case." But as I went via my possessions and got rid of the topics which have been not useful or massive to me, I felt a weight lifting off my shoulders.

I now not felt weighed down by way of the use of my possessions, but instead felt liberated through the gap and simplicity that came with having an awful lot less. I started out out to realize the things that during truth mattered to me, like spending time with loved ones, pursuing my passions, and experiencing the beauty of nature.

Living with less additionally supposed that I had more time and strength to recognition on the things that certainly mattered. I now not spent my weekends wandering via stores or scrolling through online shopping web sites. Instead, I placed pride in easy pleasures like taking a stroll within the park or cooking a meal with easy, close by components.

One non-public example of this turn out to be once I decided to sell my vehicle and begin biking to art work. I have become involved earlier than the whole lot, concerned about how I may additionally want to manipulate in terrible climate or if I had to deliver some issue heavy. But as I had been given used to the ordinary, I found that biking to art work now not most effective stored me coins on fuel and parking, however it moreover gave me a experience of freedom and independence that I had in no manner skilled in advance than.

Living with less moreover meant that I had extra monetary freedom. By saving money on needless purchases and focusing at the topics that in reality mattered, I became able to preserve up for subjects that I sincerely favored, like excursion or making an investment in my schooling. And because I modified into no longer beholden to my possessions, I felt greater assured in my potential to address something life threw my manner.

The delight of dwelling with less isn't always some aspect that can be without problems quantified or measured. It is a sense that comes from a enjoy of reason and contentment that is going past material possessions. It is a manner of dwelling that values reports over subjects, and that acknowledges the beauty and ease that may be placed in the regular.

As I maintain on my adventure of frugalism, I am constantly reminded of the pride that comes from dwelling with loads tons much less. It is a lesson that I will deliver with me for the relaxation of my lifestyles.

The Power of Budgeting

When I first started my frugal adventure, I had a indistinct concept that I needed to hold coins and reduce lower once more on my spending. However, it wasn't till I discovered the strength of budgeting that I without a doubt started out to make development.

A price range is a powerful device in order to let you take control of your price range, in preference to feeling like your price range are controlling you. It entails monitoring your earnings and fees, and developing a plan for the way you may allocate your cash each month.

One of the biggest advantages of budgeting is that it helps you to perceive regions in which you may reduce returned in your spending. By monitoring your prices, you could see precisely wherein your coins goes and perceive any regions of overspending. This permit you to make more aware alternatives approximately the way you spend your cash, and make sure which you are prioritizing your dreams and values.

For instance, once I began tracking my expenses, I found out that I grow to be spending masses of cash on consuming out and takeout meals. While I loved the gain and style of eating place meals, I found out that I have become overspending on some aspect that I want to effortlessly do myself. So I commenced out cooking greater at domestic, which not handiest stored me coins however moreover allowed me to test with new recipes and flavors.

Another gain of budgeting is that it can help you plan for the destiny. By allocating cash closer to monetary financial financial savings or paying down debt, you may create a strong basis in your financial destiny. For example, as soon as I created my first price variety, I made first-rate to include a line item for emergency financial savings. While I did not understand precisely what I might need the cash for, I knew that having a cushion would probable offer me peace of thoughts and shield me in case of unexpected charges.

Finally, budgeting can be empowering. When you've got a plan for your cash, you sense extra on top of things of your rate variety and can make intentional options approximately the way you want to stay your existence. You can keep for topics which can be vital to you, like a holiday or a modern-day vehicle, and feel confident which you are making development within the course of your desires.

One private example of this end up when I decided to go yet again to highschool to pursue a modern-day career. While the idea of taking on more debt changed into daunting, I knew that through manner of creating a finances and making intentional alternatives about my spending, I must make it paintings. By lowering lower back on useless fees and allocating coins closer to training bills, I modified into able to advantage my purpose of incomes a diploma without sacrificing my financial stability.

In forestall, the strength of budgeting can not be overstated. It is a clean however powerful device that permit you to take control of your finances, plan for the destiny, and make intentional selections about the manner you need to live your lifestyles.

Chapter 15: Finding The Right Mindset

When it comes to frugalism, finding the proper thoughts-set is prime. It's no longer quite a good deal reducing lower back on your spending, but it is about developing a terrific manner of thinking about cash and sources.

For me, finding the proper mind-set intended shifting my consciousness from what I didn't have to what I did have. Instead of feeling deprived due to the truth I couldn't control to pay for the modern gadgets or cutting-edge clothes, I commenced to understand the things that I did have and find out pleasure within the clean pleasures of existence.

One way I did this end up by way of the usage of training gratitude. I started out a gratitude magazine wherein I may additionally want to write down down 3 things I emerge as thankful for every day, irrespective of how small they may seem. This helped me to shift my focus a ways from what I lacked and within the direction of the abundance in my existence, whether or not it changed right into a warmth cup of tea or a kind phrase from a pal.

Another important mindset shift for me changed into understanding that being frugal does not endorse being reasonably-priced or sacrificing first rate. Instead, it's miles about being intentional together with your spending and prioritizing the subjects that simply rely to you. For example, I like to excursion, so instead of reserving the most inexpensive possible flights and lodges, I spend time studying and locating the first-rate gives on outstanding journey reviews that healthy inner my price range.

It's moreover critical to permit move of the idea that material possessions equate to happiness. While it is able to be tempting to buy subjects a very good way to experience better or to electrify others, the reality is that material possessions quality offer transient pride. Instead, I find out fulfillment in opinions and relationships, which bring lasting happiness and reminiscences.

Finally, a frugal mind-set consists of being aware of your resources and the effect that your options have at the arena round you. This manner lowering waste, the usage of belongings successfully, and making options that align collectively along with your values. For instance, I pick to buy regionally grown produce and help small agencies, which not best reduces my carbon footprint however additionally helps to manual my nearby network.

In conclusion, finding the proper mind-set is essential for living a frugal life. It includes shifting your focus from what you lack to what you've got had been given, prioritizing the subjects that honestly depend to you, locating satisfaction in easy pleasures, and being mindful of your effect on the arena. By developing a frugal mind-set, you may find out economic freedom, fulfillment, and a deeper appreciation for the abundance to your life.

The Secret to Frugal Grocery Shopping

When it consists of frugalism, one of the maximum essential regions to focus on is grocery shopping for. After all, food is a need, and it is also one in every of the largest costs for max families. However, with a few easy techniques, it's miles possible to shop coins on groceries on the identical time as nonetheless ingesting well.

One of the critical aspect secrets and strategies to frugal grocery buying is to plot earlier. This technique creating a listing of what you need earlier than you go to the store and sticking to it. It moreover technique taking the time to look at profits flyers and coupons to find out the amazing offers. For instance, if you apprehend that fowl breasts are on sale this week, plan your meals spherical that and inventory up.

Another vital method is to buy in bulk. This does now not mean you want to visit a warehouse keep and buy a 365 days's supply of relaxation room paper, however it does endorse that you want to endure in thoughts looking for large portions of gadgets which you use regularly. For instance, if you devour oatmeal every morning, purchasing for a huge subject of oats is in all likelihood more price-effective than seeking out man or woman packets.

It's additionally vital to keep in mind of in that you save. While it can be tempting to do all your purchasing at one hold for comfort, one of a kind stores frequently have specific expenses and profits. For example, I discover that my community grocery maintain has the best charges on produce, but the close by farmer's marketplace has outstanding gives on meat and dairy.

When it includes the real shopping for adventure, there are some recommendations a good way to will can help you maintain cash. First, keep with a complete stomach to avoid impulse purchases. Second, attempt to preserve on with the edge of the shop, in which the easy produce, meat, and dairy are positioned, in place of the middle aisles wherein the processed and packaged elements are placed. Finally, remember shopping for store manufacturers in choice to call manufacturers. In regularly, the exceptional is the identical, however the charge is decrease.

One personal example of the manner I keep cash on groceries is thru meal making plans. At the begin of the week, I sit down down and plan out what food I'll be making for the week, based totally on what I have already got in my pantry and what is on sale at the shop. I make a listing of all the elements I'll need and then stick with that list once I buy groceries. By doing this, I'm capable of keep away from last-minute takeout orders and wasted meals, which allows me preserve coins in the end.

In end, frugal grocery buying is all about making plans earlier, looking for in bulk, being aware of in which you hold, and making smart choices in the store. By following these techniques, you could store cash to your grocery bill at the equal time as nonetheless eating nicely and taking detail in scrumptious food.

Meal Planning on a Tight Budget

One of the simplest methods to hold coins on meals is through meal making plans. By planning out your meals earlier, you could keep strategically, keep away from final-minute takeout orders, and reduce meals waste. However, on the identical time as you are on a excellent budget, meal planning can appear to be a frightening mission. But worry not, there are masses of strategies to devise food on a rate variety with out sacrificing taste or nutrients.

The first step in meal planning on a first rate finances is to take stock of what you have got already got on your pantry and refrigerator. This will allow you to avoid looking for elements which you do no longer want and to dissipate objects which may be close to their expiration date. Once what you have got got, you could start to devise your food for the week.

When making plans food on a finances, it's far critical to reputation on less expensive, nutrient-dense additives. This approach incorporating plenty of prevent cease result, veggies, entire grains, and lean protein assets into your food. It's additionally vital to be aware of detail sizes and to avoid losing meals. Leftovers may be repurposed for lunch day after today or frozen for destiny meals.

Another key technique is to buy substances in bulk. This may be particularly price-effective for staples like grains, beans, and nuts. By buying in bulk, you can keep coins and make certain which you continually have the ones components reachable even as you need them.

One private instance of the way I plan food on a price range is thru the usage of the use of the "put together dinner as fast as, eat two times" method. For instance, if I'm growing a pot of chili, I'll make a double batch and freeze 1/2 for later. This no longer first rate saves cash on substances however additionally saves time on meal prep inside the future.

Another private method is to use seasonal produce. In-season produce is regularly an awful lot less pricey and tastes higher than out-of-season produce that desires to be shipped from some distance away. I additionally try and store at neighborhood farmer's markets, wherein I can frequently find a whole lot less high-priced, easy produce.

When it involves the real meal making plans method, I find out it beneficial to devise meals round factors which is probably on sale that week. I furthermore attempt to plan food that uses similar elements, really so I can buy in bulk and use elements in multiple foods.

In end, meal planning on a first rate finances can be hard, but it's miles now not not possible. By specializing in low rate, nutrient-dense components, looking for in bulk, and being aware of food waste, you could keep cash in your grocery invoice and despite the fact that enjoy delicious and nutritious food. With a bit little bit of planning and creativity, meal making plans on a respectable price range can grow to be a a laugh and profitable a part of your frugal manner of life.

Reducing Waste and Saving Money

In a global wherein waste is so common, it's far crucial to make an effort to reduce it each time viable. Not only is that this accurate for the surroundings, however it is able to moreover save you coins ultimately. Here are some hints and private examples for reducing waste and saving coins to your each day existence.

One of an appropriate techniques to reduce waste is to keep your very very personal reusable luggage while buying. This can consist of reusable grocery luggage, produce luggage, or maybe shopping baggage for distinctive sorts of shops. By the use of reusable baggage, you could keep away from the use of single-use plastic baggage that emerge as in landfills or oceans.

Another manner to reduce waste is to apply reusable bins for meals storage. Instead of the usage of disposable plastic luggage or packing containers, pick reusable containers product of glass or metal. These can be used over and over once more, and might help lessen the amount of waste you generate.

When it entails food waste, meal planning is an crucial approach. By making plans your food earlier and shopping for simplest what you need, you could reduce the amount of food this is going to waste. This can save you money in your grocery invoice and reduce the amount of meals that in the end ends up in landfills.

Another manner to lessen food waste is to compost. Composting is a natural manner that breaks down herbal materials like meals scraps and yard waste into nutrient-wealthy soil. By composting, you can lessen the quantity of waste this is going into landfills and create your private fertilizer on your garden or houseplants. I in my opinion began composting after I observed about the benefits of it and the way smooth it is to do. Now, I enjoy suitable knowledge that I'm no longer throwing away food scraps and other natural waste, and as an alternative the use of them to create some aspect useful.